KALEIDOSCOPE

PROJECTS AND IDEAS TO
SPARK YOUR CREATIVITY

suzanne simanaitis

NORTH LIGHT BOOKS
CINCINNATI, OHIO
WWW.ARTISTSNETWORK.COM

Kaleidoscope Copyright (c) 2007 by Suzanne Simanaitis. Manufactured in China. All rights reserved. The patterns and drawings in the book are for personal use of reader. By permission of the author and publisher, they may be either hand-traced or photocopied to make single copies, but under no circumstances may they be resold or republished. It is permissible for the purchaser to make the projects contained herein and sell them at fairs, bazaars and craft shows. No other part of this book may be reproduced in any form or by any electronic or mechanical means including information storage and retrieval systems without permission in writing from the publisher, except by a reviewer, who may quote a brief passage in review. Published by North Light Books, an imprint of F+W Publications, Inc., 4700 East Galbraith Road, Cincinnati, Ohio 45236. (800) 289-0963. First edition.

11 10 09 08 07   5 4 3 2 1

Distributed in Canada by Fraser Direct
100 Armstrong Avenue
Georgetown, ON, Canada L7G 5S4
Tel: (905) 877-4411

Distributed in the U.K. and Europe by David & Charles
Brunel House, Newton Abbot, Devon, TQ12 4PU, England
Tel: (+44) 1626 323200, Fax: (+44) 1626 323319
Email: postmaster@davidandcharles.co.uk

Distributed in Australia by Capricorn Link
P.O. Box 704, S. Windsor, NSW 2756 Australia
Tel: (02) 4577-3555

Library of Congress Cataloging-in-Publication Data

Simanaitis, Suzanne.
  Kaleidoscope : projects and ideas to spark your creativity / Suzanne Simanaitis.
      p. cm.
  Includes index.
  ISBN-13: 978-1-58180-879-7 (pbk. : alk. paper)
  ISBN-10: 1-58180-879-8 (pbk. : alk. paper)
  1. Art--Technique. 2. Improvisation in art. 3. Art--Psychology. I. Title.
  N7430.S496 2006
  702.8--dc22

      2006017206

Editor: Tonia Davenport
Cover and Interior Designer: Karla Baker
Production Coordinator: Greg Nock
Photographer: Christine Polomsky

fw
F+W PUBLICATIONS, INC.

about Suzanne

Suzanne Simanaitis has been a crafty girl all along but, as far as she knows, it only recently began to alarm her friends and family. She's not worried about it. Suz lives and loves in the cutest little house in Hawthorne, California, where she makes stuff and publishes *ARTitude Zine*, an independent magazine about art, craft and creativity. Her perfect day would include Hawkeye Pierce, brownies à la mode and a karaoke machine. Send her mail art and she'll be your friend for life, and in the meantime, pay a visit to www.artitudezine.com.

COVER ART CONTRIBUTORS:

Bernie Berlin
Sarah Fishburn
Miranda Hempel
Cathy Mendola
Suzanne Simanaitis

DEDICATION

This book is lovingly dedicated to the ARTitude Zine creative community, and to Helga Strauss, with whom I first dreamed it. I am buoyed by what we accomplish together!

This book is a manifestation of the lively spirit in which zine makers and zine readers share their interests, questions and journeys. Any and all juiciness must be attributed to the art and ideas so generously shared by its many talented contributors, whom I profusely thank for their efforts and their trust.

I'd like to thank Mom for showering me with pearls of wisdom, and Dad for living the truth that work can be fun; Maria for circles; Randi for perspective; TL for spark; and Vivian for "Yes, and ..."

Tonia Davenport, your patient and joyful handling of the material and this first-time book author made all the difference.

At the height of laughter, the universe is flung into a kaleidoscope of new possibilities.
~ Jean Houston

Wednesdays child became self obsessed and pushy in order to stay at the top and wouldnt even give herself a break.

CONTENTS

artwork on this page:
DEBRA BIANCHI, CHARLOTTE KEMSLEY, NIKKI BLACKWOOD, PILAR POLLOCK, WENDY COOK, JULIE SADLER, SUZANNE SIMANAITIS, JULIANA COLES, ROBIN OLSEN, MARY HALDEMAN

Passionately Curious?

I have no special talents. I am only passionately curious.

~Albert Einstein

Hi.

My name is Suz, and I am the passionately curious person who put this book together for you. Wow, already this is not sounding like a typical book—and it shouldn't! I'm not a professional writer or teacher; I'm an artsy-craftsy dabbler and independent publisher, and right now I'd like you to think of me as your creative cruise director, the splashy interior decorator who's come to wallpaper a corner of your mind. A couple dozen talented friends and I created this book—a collection of projects, ideas and artwork culled from the thriving art zine scene—to nourish the artist in you.

"Me, an artist?"

Yes—does it not spill easily from your lips? Do you harbor a secret belief that artists are weird or irresponsible or, well, *different*? The truth is that there can be art in any type of endeavor. The key is to approach your work (and your play!) with an open mind that welcomes any possibility and embraces any outcome. The artistry is in choosing which possibilities to leave in and which to toss out, and you learn to make those decisions by practicing. Being an artist means never being bored, because your innate curiosity keeps you asking questions and exploring. And when the trail you blaze

artwork at left:
DEBRA BIANCHI, MELISSA MCCOBB HUBBELL, PILAR POLLOCK, ELSIE SAMPSON, LOU MCCULLOCH, TERRY LEE GETZ

brings you to the edge of what you think is possible, you keep going and try something different, just to see what happens . . .

"So ... if I'm an artist, should I be into watercolor or oils?"

As if those were the only choices! How about packing tape, beeswax and an egg timer? Because that's just a hint of what's in store for you in this book. Even the articles based on relatively traditional art media like collage and photography include some kind of twist. Zine writers are like jazz musicians: they take a familiar idea and add their own special flair by introducing different textures, unexpected techniques and a fresh personal perspective. Sometimes these improvised riffs take the form of how-to projects while others are more like extended solos where you can sit back, put your feet up and enjoy the music. Either way, we hope they'll inspire you to take part in our art zine jam session.

"Right . . . um, what the heck is a zine?"

I thought you'd never ask! A zine (pronounced *zeen*, short for "magazine") is a small independent publication. Beyond that, there really aren't too many rules.

In this book we'll draw upon art and creativity-related zines, but there are people who produce zines on any and every topic you can imagine. The first zine I ever read was about Evel Knievel. I wasn't particularly interested in Evel Knievel (a motorcycle daredevil whose greatest days were already distant in history's rearview mirror), but the author's zealous approach to his topic sucked me in. I was intrigued that this guy was so obsessed with Evel Knievel that he had volumes to say about him and an urgent desire to share his knowledge with others. In that sense, the art zines represented in this book are not all that different from the Evel Knievel zine. We're just passionately curious about art, craft and creative exchange instead of crazy over a flashy 1970s stuntman.

"Okay, wait — how does Evel Knievel fit in?"

He doesn't. Forget I mentioned him because, despite that author's fervent attempt to convert me, it turned out that I wasn't able to sustain a passion for all things Evel. I am zealous about art zines, and I hope you will be, too.

Although rough around the edges, every zine has its charm. Zines in a small format draw you into their confidential embrace, and large ones can bowl you over with all the energy they release when you tear open that envelope.

Some zines are handwritten and reproduced on the sly during lunch hour on the office copier. You know you're dealing with a hardcore do-it-yourself zine maker when you meet someone who owns a long-neck stapler, essential for securing the folded booklets. Other zines are professionally printed and bound, but even the spiffy-looking ones still display a healthy dose

of their creators' genuine personalities. While a glossy, nationally distributed "real" magazine must appeal to a broad swath of the market to remain commercially viable, a zine has the freedom to just be itself, because its reason for being is not about making money—it's about having a conversation, a give-and-take of ideas and inspiration with a small but devoted audience.

A few of the zines represented in this book measure their circulation in dozens while others achieve distribution numbers of a thousand copies or more. Most consider themselves comfortably successful with a couple hundred readers. Nobody gets rich by publishing a zine. We're lucky and grateful if we break even on the printing and postage costs, and our only reimbursement is the satisfaction of hearing from enthusiastic readers, many of whom eventually summon their courage to become enthusiastic contributors of artwork and ideas.

"So, what does this zine stuff have to do with this book?"

This book is essentially like a great big zine—unusual in that it enjoys the luxury of being printed in glorious full color, yet typical in that it represents the creative input of a diverse group of contributors. Like many zines, the book is organized around themes with multiple voices communicating different aspects of a single topic. A handful of the pieces in this book were originally published in zines, but most were written specifically for this project.

One of the nicest comments I've heard about my publication, *ARTitude Zine*, was from a woman who told me that when she reads it she feels like she is playing with friends in a secret treehouse. There is something personal and intimate about a zine, something immediate and compelling about the communication that happens in its pages. A zine tends to be closely identified with the voice of its creator, there's no screen of formality between the writer and the audience and it is assumed that they are on a shared wavelength. Zines are passed from person to person like a secret handshake. "Here, this might look a little odd to some, but I think you'll get it," we wink. Readers and contributors feel understood within the embrace of a favorite zine, and these are circumstances that encourage creativity to flourish.

"Oh good, I like to flourish!"

Then let's get started! The following chapters are succulent and are filled with the best of what art zines offer: tempting projects, imaginative essays and juicy artwork to inspire and motivate your hands, heart and mind.

As you try various techniques in this book, please bring a sense of yourself to the process. That is, don't feel like you have to make a project exactly as it is described here. If the instructions call for an accordion-folded book but you'd rather use a book with a traditional left-hand spine, go right ahead and use what you want. Later, if it turns out that there was, in fact, a rather good reason to use the specific thing listed, then congratulations! Artistic minds thrive on problem-solving exercises like the one you just created. Hop to it!

Consider each project, opinion and anecdote to be a jumping-off point for your unique imagination. For years I felt disappointed in myself because I didn't enjoy making collages out of magazine clippings—and as you will see in later chapters, this process is an extremely powerful creative manifestation tool in certain people's hands! I eventually realized that I feel intimidated by the energetic layouts that are typical of that approach. I process information best when it builds up in layers and everything has its own little space, it's too overwhelming for me to see everything promiscuously mingling. As soon as I understood this key factor about how I learn, I was able to tweak creative projects to suit the way my brain works. I hope that if one of our suggestions isn't a good fit for you, you will allow your curiosity to examine that reaction and discover an alternate strategy that suits you.

By the way, nothing in this book can teach you how to be creative. You already are creative. The trick is to allow that playful impulse to blossom, and this book just might be helpful in that regard. You bring the curious mind and willing hands, and let the collected wisdom of our contributors supply the games, ideas and projects that will encourage you to stretch in new directions as an artist.

"Then why isn't this book called The Magic and Wisdom of Art Zines?"

Well, because two pages ago, did you even know what an art zine was? The title of this book, *Kaleidoscope*, translates from the original Greek as "beautiful form" and is defined as "a series of changing phases." In the first of many things about "real" publishing that I found surprising during the process of compiling this book, I didn't get to choose the name. But it turns out that "kaleidoscope" is a darn good description of an art zine and of the collection of things you'll find here. A zine undoubtedly will grow and change over the course of its lifespan as its creator acquires new tools and new interests. Also, its audience develops new skills and an expanded creative vocabulary, and together their evolution is reflected in the pages of the publication.

The operative word—*reflected*—a kaleidoscope uses mirrors inside a tube to reflect constantly shifting patterns of colors and shapes, and a zine mirrors the vibrant and restless minds of the fluid group of people who contribute to its pages. Now it's your turn to peer through this Kaleidoscope. Let its colorful contents tumble around to form new shapes, and see what emerges from your unique perspective.

Over thirty passionately curious artists lend their talents to this book. Many of them publish their own art zines, and you can learn more about those at the end of the book. I hope you'll check them out and get in on the vibrant conversations already underway!

Have fun and flourish.

Suz

he song
ng that
it is a
and desire.
e love of life

that is the quest
the hopes and
dreams that
I have locked
away, do they
dare to make
their way t
the surface
do I dare
speak t
words th
come fro
the feel
locked a

sings
rom
d
long

Married

Pieces of Me

Who am I? I am a wife, a
mother, a daughter, an artist,
a teacher, a musician, a
friend, a student, and things
that have not yet revealed
themselves to me. I am more
than my body, my thoughts,
my experiences, my passions,
and my fears. I am a work in
progress. I am a divine soul;
part of a greater tapestry of
other divine souls —Beings of
Light. I am here to evolve
into my best self —to come to
trust in the Universe, learn
from adverse experiences,
and revel in as much joy as I
possibly can in this lifetime

...TITY

If you do not tell the truth about yourself you cannot tell it about other people.

~Virginia Woolf

In claiming the identity o... ...ve, sweet self, be bold about ... ...o dive in, it is actually safest to a...

The first time I told so... ...tist," it sounded so strange. The ... ...were out, I felt I should retract th... ...fy them by adding, "… but not... ... "I'm an artist but I can't draw or p... ...st but only in my spare time." But o... ...fied by a martini and a resolve to t...y on a new attitude, I left it at "I am an artist." And you know what happened? Much to my surprise, the Art Police didn't storm the place to take me into custody, charging me with impersonating an artist. Nobody averted their eyes from my dazzling brilliance, either, or scattered fragrant rose petals in my path. A simple declarative statement, "I am an artist," floated before me, calmly blinking yet invisible to my conversation partner, for me alone to consider. Ever since that night, I have examined and challenged my assumptions about who I am and have become more confident about my ability to alter and interpret each momentary reality.

We use colors, shapes and images that originate outside us as our building blocks, but if all we are doing is stacking them into a neat pile—background, frame, focal point, accent—there is something missing. That missing element is a spark, the uniqueness, the voice. It's the difference, some would argue, between craft and art. The craftsperson is skilled, certainly; she knows the capabilities of her materials, and when she begins her process she knows what she wants to achieve. The

artist isn't sure where her process may lead. As artists, we explore the unknown while craftspeople tend to stick to the known. Artists clarify relationships between design elements to communicate ideas via our work. Perhaps by practicing this relationship-building process in collage, assemblage or writing, you'll arrive at the blossoming of a more comfortable relationship between you and the artist you are becoming.

As Susan Tuttle does on page 20, ask yourself, "Who am I?" and see what answers come to mind. Make a list of them—daughter, caretaker, business owner, alto. Write down "artist" and see how that makes you feel. Empowered? Anxious? Like a case of mistaken identity? Reshape the list into a map and see how the various versions of you are interrelated or isolated. Think about what you'd like your identity map to look like in five years, or twenty.

The articles in this chapter are about identity, as each author comes to know something about herself by exploring relationships: with her appearance, her companions, her inner world, her environment. Does that sound a little scary? This is one cool thing that zines can do. Zine makers are not Great Thinkers or anything. We're just curious people who are unafraid to ask great questions, and we wield our art tools in ways we hope will begin to define some answers. A zine is a great place to get an idea onto the page and out there in front of a small but appreciative audience. In doing this, we declare, "This is who I am right now, and this is where I am with my expression of it. What do you say?" It floats there, calmly blinking. And the conversation begins.

artwork at left:
KATE LYON, MARLEE FOSBRE, COREY MOORTGAT
SUSAN TUTTLE, RANDI FEUERHELM-WATTS

A Magnificent Obsession

BY CLAUDIA MEDARIS

I have this ongoing daydream where I construct My Ideal Life: I'm four inches taller (taller than my daughters), six years younger (younger than my little sister), restored to my fighting weight (move over, Kate Moss), earning a handsome living authoring a series of historical mysteries (traveling to Italy every summer for research, of course), while maintaining a fluid and open conduit to my Muse (writing is effortless, nearly automatic), under a pseudonym to preserve my privacy, with a mane of carelessly tossed, sun-touched hair setting off a perfect tan. (There's no room in this fantasy for a shabby dust jacket photo.)

In the midst of all this, my husband has transformed into an important and respected romantic poet. (In reality, he does love poetry.) When I think about it, I could be quite happy with these few small adjustments—after all, I've spent over half a century coping with the haphazard way things have been set up by the powers-that-be and a more-random-than-is-desired gene pool. We can produce designer drugs, so why not designer lives?

Okay ... Y-e-e-e-s, if you're going to get realistic on me, certainly I could have "lived up to my potential" and made this fantasy more of a reality. I could have (a) applied myself, (b) worked harder, (c) taken calculated risks or (d) "put myself out there" ... in short, if I'd concentrated. I'll be the first to admit the blueprint of my existence is my fault entirely. Somehow, life got in the way; small things became big hurdles early on, and wow—they turned into humongous things. Who knew that could happen? High school counselors don't tell you that's possible, do they? Oh, they do? I guess I wasn't concentrating.

Looking about for examples of artists who did concentrate, I picked up Diane Middlebrook's *Her Husband: Hughes and Plath, a Marriage*, and while reading this, it occured to me that besides framing a convincing argument for Ted Hughes not being the antifeminist evildoer our Women's Literature professors in the 1970s would have led us to believe, Middlebrook would like us to come away with how Sylvia Plath and Ted Hughes bullheadedly constructed their lives. They were obsessed with becoming poets. Dank, minuscule apartments and crying babies, money worries, extramarital alliances inducing over-the-top fits of jealousy and serious mental illnesses were not allowed to become impediments.

Theirs was a blended, artistic marriage, an entanglement of psyches linked on a cosmic level, their dancing minds entwined in a double helix of creative fire. In a few short years, they shot up the

ladder of poetic greatness together. Granted, in an equally short span of time, their marriage and, not incidentally, Sylvia's life were sacrificed. Things fell apart rather spectacularly, but they made a hell of a lot of art together before the end came.

It's that creative togetherness in their partnership I find inspiring. Their interplay of creativity reached rare levels of equality as they nurtured shared poetic themes. One was not merely a helpmate; one, not only a mentor. Obviously, as time passed, Ted could have lent a hand around the house, arranged to heat their apartment, and maybe not screwed around so much, but hey, they created together equally, the large body of their work echoing down to us today in beautifully haunting call-and-response refrains. Decades after Plath's death, Hughes was still embedding the mutual poetic themes of their cosmic collaboration in his work.

Personally, I'm a bit unfamiliar with how the landscape of a creative partnership might be navigated. My husband prefers to think "he is a rock, he is an i-i-i-island …" (thank you, Paul Simon) and is the type who would no more write alongside me for several hours each morning than take it upon himself to design

storage shelving for my studio or tag along and hold my bags while I shop obsessively at a RubberRama. He's busy with motherboards and interfaces and … things. To be fair, I'm sure I'm not much of a techie partner from his standpoint either, since my main computer skill is jamming the printer and whining.

While my husband is obsessed with electronics and cyberspace, Sylvia Plath's was obsessed with astrology, mythology and Robert Graves's *The White Goddess*. Sounds romantic and cool, huh? However, seeing as how not one but two of Hughes's partners committed suicide, having a right-brained husband may not be quite the creative Eden it's cracked up to be.

Maybe I'll stop obsessing about my "ideal life" and have another look at what reality doled out to me one lucky day about twenty years ago. My husband may not sit by the fire and write verse with me, but he has enjoyed Robert Graves himself, has great taste in classical music and literature, makes us a mean martini every Friday night, and is a practiced absorber of my particular brand of whining. A lot of artistic women make do with a lot less.

CONCEIVING
a work of art

✳ BY COREY MOORTGAT ✳

You will find a small fortune.

Baby

DEVELOPMENT OF THE

Baby Moortgat

CECROPIA MOTH

03/07/2005

As any mother can tell you, the journey of a first-time pregnancy is a roller-coaster ride—from the decision to try and conceive, to the heartbreak of failed attempts, to the excitement of the positive pregnancy test, and finally to the mystery of the pregnancy itself. Being an artist, I naturally wanted to document these life-changing events. So on April 6, 2004, I began what would become both an amazing journey in my life as well as an intensely personal body of artwork.

Until that point, my artwork had been moving toward a more personal, journal-istic style. I created an art journal about my wedding the previous year, and it seemed that even when I didn't intend it, the art pieces I produced always had personal meaning by the time I was finished with them. So when my husband and I decided it was time to start a family, I made a piece of art to commemorate it. I wrote about the dream I'd had that facilitated the discussion and about my emotions surrounding the decision. I used images of babies and families and birds and nests.

And so began my "pregnancy journal." The first few entries were wistful and optimistic. I was so excited about having a baby, I was sure that I'd be pregnant within a couple months. I did a piece about seeing a rainbow and wondering whether it was a "sign" I was pregnant, and one about a fortune cookie that said, "You will receive a small fortune." Two months into trying, but still feeling positive, I did a piece about some experiences we'd had that seemed as if they were reminding us to be patient.

But gradually, the art became more and more depressed. Not being close to anyone who had tried becoming pregnant, I hadn't realized what a slow, difficult process it could be. Those two weeks after each ovulation were soooo long, and only to be disappointed month after month. Each piece of art seemed to say the same thing: "Another month and no baby." Words like "stationary," "hindered," "empty" and "detained" crept into the art. After many failed attempts, I began feeling

14

like I would never become pregnant. But, as hard as the journey was becoming, I needed to keep up with the journal. It was important to continue the story, because I was still hopeful that I would be able to see it through to a happy ending. It wouldn't be a truthful story if I only documented the happy times.

Finally, twelve pieces of art and ten months later, the happy ending (or is it the beginning?) arrived: I was pregnant! I was simultaneously ecstatic and scared to death that something bad might happen. The first piece of art I did was a painting of a nude woman with "hanging by a thread" written in the womb area. This was how I felt the first few days—like the pregnancy was so delicate, it could end at any second. Not a very positive thought! But a few days later I began to regret not having created a "happy" piece of art when I found out the good news, so I did another "I'm pregnant!" piece which shows a laughing baby and the word "blossom." It's quite interesting to look at the two pieces together. The first is very muted and quiet, whereas the second is colorful and has much more movement. Both of them accurately reflect the emotions I was having during those beginning stages of the pregnancy.

When I did the next piece, I was still feeling anxious so I collaged two angels to watch over and protect the baby. Slowly, though, I started feeling more confident, and the artwork became more colorful and optimistic. I created art about the first ultrasound, hearing the heartbeat for the first time, learning that we were having a boy (Oh dear! Coming from a family of three girls, what would I do with a boy?), decorating the nursery, and the impatience and excitement of waiting for the birth. At last, nine months and twelve more pieces of art later, we had our beautiful baby boy, Riley Brennan!

In addition to a baby, I had created twenty-four pieces of art. When I began the process, my intent was to frame each piece and hang them in chronological order in the nursery, but twenty-four was a few too many to fit! So I chose four of my favorites (including the first "I'm pregnant!" piece—surprisingly, it has become one of my favorites because of its raw honesty) and framed them. This left me with twenty loose pieces. Not wanting them to get damaged, I decided to bind them together into a book.

I didn't mention earlier that Riley enjoyed his time in my tummy so much that he was eight days overdue. During that extremely long week after his due date, I began sewing each collage onto a piece of fabric. Then, each piece of fabric was sandwiched between shelf paper (for easy cleaning and durability)

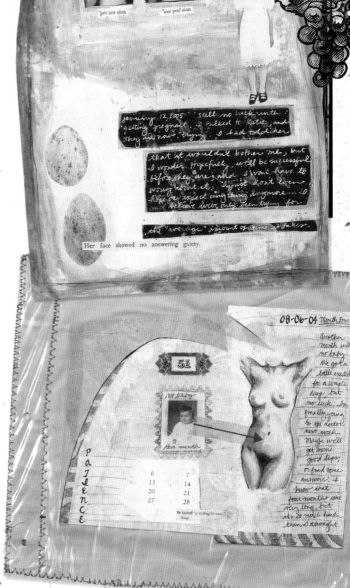

and clear vinyl and sewn around the edge. This made for tedious work: perfect when you're trying to keep your mind on anything but a late baby! I sewed a fabric cover, and my husband attached the mechanism from a three-ring binder to the inside to hold the "pages." This way, I'll be able to add the four artworks that are hanging in his room at a later date, keeping them in the correct order. I also

enclosed, safe place for a little bird. The same would be true of a nest or an egg. So the birds, I guess, are representations of my husband, of me, and sometimes of the baby.

Another theme that emerged is that of the number three. Many of the pieces show groupings of three: three birds, three babies, three main subjects in the piece. The significance of "three" is obvious: our family was growing from two members to three members. What's really interesting is that even collages I created during this time that weren't part of this series seemed to have the number three figured prominently too. In fact, most of my art done during these months ended up being about the pregnancy in one way or another, regardless of whether I intended it or not.

Looking over the collages one day, I noticed that one of the pieces was created on January 12, 2005, which, according to my calculations, was probably the day on which my son was conceived. Interested to see what I had written that day, I looked more closely at the piece. I had written about my sister, who had just informed me that she and her husband were trying to get pregnant. The images I had used in the art were two similar photos of a little boy (unusual for me because I almost always use images of girls instead of boys), two

attached a handle to the side, and the book now hangs from a hook on the side of Riley's dresser, right next to the rocking chair.

Now that I'm not immersed in the pregnancy anymore, I can sit in the chair and look at the journal (between feedings and changings, of course!). It's really interesting to see all the pieces together in one place, because as I was creating them, I was only seeing one piece, one moment at a time. Now I see the emergence of themes, symbols and amazing stories that I hadn't noticed before.

One motif that is very present in the group is that of birds, eggs, nests and birdcages. Someone recently asked what significance the birdcages hold for me. Although I could say that I just like the graphic element of the thin, rhythmic lines that represent the wires of the cage, I know that, subconsciously, there's more to it. I've always used shapes like arches and shrines in my work (and these shapes are abundant in this series of artworks as well) because they feel safe and enveloping to me. The birdcage is another form of this shape, with a more literal meaning. To me, the birdcage is like a womb: an

eggs, and two birdcages. Strangely, I had used "twos" in this piece instead of "threes." I was absolutely amazed. You see, it turned out that my sister and I both became pregnant on the same day, and we both delivered boys nine months later!

Obviously, this body of work holds a lot of meaning for me. Aside from my beautiful baby, it's the greatest thing I've ever created. I envision us looking at the book together in a few years, and I imagine telling him the story of how Mommy and Daddy wanted a baby so much, and of how he grew in my tummy for nine months (plus one week, the little stinker!). Of course, I may be dreaming to think that a little boy is going to be at all interested in this journal, but I'm confident that one day he will fully appreciate it, even if it's not until he is trying to start a family of his own. And if not, that's okay; I did the artwork for myself. Every time I look at a piece, I'm transported to the day I created it. For me it's both a photo album and a diary. This book encapsulates almost two years of my life—two of the most intense and life-changing years I've experienced to date. I'm so glad that I have something substantial I can actually hold in my hands to remember this time. It's a treasure that I hope will last forever!

REFLECTION DECK

BY MARILEE FOSBRE

SEVERAL YEARS AGO I LOOKED AROUND MY STUDIO AT ALL THE PROJECTS I HAD CREATED AND DECIDED THAT I WANTED TO MOVE BEYOND MASTERING THE LATEST TECHNIQUES OR COPYING THE ART I ADMIRED IN MAGAZINES. I LONGED TO FOCUS INWARD AND TO EXPRESS MYSELF THROUGH UNIQUELY PERSONAL ART. SINCE THAT DAY I HAVE HEADED DOWN A DIFFERENT PATH, ONE OF IMAGES, WORDS AND SELF-EXPLORATION. THE REFLECTION DECK GREW OUT OF THIS JOURNEY. WHAT BETTER WAY TO CREATE UNIQUE ART THAN BY USING PERSONAL PHOTOS? EACH PICTURE IS A TIME CAPSULE OF MEMORIES, EMOTIONS, DREAMS AND DESIRES.

Because you are making the deck just for yourself and using photos of only yourself, a Reflection Deck is a very personal and empowering way to silence your inner critic and lose yourself in art. The cards in this deck are powerful works of art that speak directly from your heart, resonating in an unexpected and rewarding way. Each card can stand alone as a private and evocative small collage piece, or the cards can be combined as a deck and used to explore and reveal inner knowledge.

To get started, scavenge through those old shoe boxes and dresser drawers to unearth your stash of photos. Try to gather photos of yourself at all ages and stages of your life. Scan or photocopy the pictures and put the originals back where you found them so they will be there the next time you need them. This is not the time to get organized—you can do that when you're seventy. Print the copied photos on text-weight paper and cut away the backgrounds (literally and figuratively)—including ex-husbands, siblings, old houses, front lawns and Christmas trees—until you have just the images of you remaining.

Gather these images into a pile and play with them for a while; spend some time looking at each one and reflecting about that time in your life. What was your name then? What did people call you? What did you call yourself? What did you need? Who did you love? Who loved you? What were your dreams? These are just a few of the questions you may decide to explore as you are creating your cards.

Married Woman

Reflection Deck cards are simple collages with the image of you as the focal point. Before you start, decide how big you want the finished deck to be. You can either assemble your collages within that dimension or work on a larger surface and then reduce the originals on a photocopier to create the final deck. I create 5" × 7" (13cm × 18cm) originals and reduce them by 50 percent to end up with a deck that is 2½" × 3½" (6cm × 9cm), a size that fits nicely in your hand as well as into standard, trading-card storage sleeves.

For the backgrounds, use paint, bits of torn paper, magazine images, text and numbers. Layer the elements on watercolor paper or any other paper that will hold up to the materials you are using. I like to make large, sloppy background papers and then cut them into 5" × 7" (13cm × 18cm) panels. Adhere an image of you onto a background and then add text and images on top. Think about the questions that you asked yourself as you were playing with the images and add elements to the collage to answer those questions.

When the collages are finished, reduce them on a photocopier to the desired size (unless, of course, you created them at that size). Print or copy them onto card-stock instead of paper so they will hold up to frquent handling. Choose a pleasing patterned paper as a backing and glue it to the reverse of the cardstock. Then cut out the cards and use a corner rounding punch on the corners.

Keep a supply of cutout images of you in a cigar box and add to it when more photos surface. If you have only a few suitable photos of yourself, you can create an infinite variety of photocopies to use by enlarging, reducing and manipulating the photos when you copy them; try cropping only your mouth or eyes for cards about significant things you've said or seen. Throw in relevant words or phrases you find in magazines or old books. Save the scrap papers that line your art table and discarded parts of unfinished projects; use them as quick background layers for your cards.

Making a Reflection Deck card is a great way to jumpstart your creativity when you feel stuck or self-critical. Just pull out these saved elements and create a card. Before you know it you'll be on the path of your own personal journey.

EXPLORING THE LANDSCAPE WITHIN

a Self-Portrait

BY SUSAN TUTTLE

ASK YOURSELF THE QUESTION. "WHO AM I?" WHAT IS YOUR IMMEDIATE RESPONSE? AS YOU PONDER THE QUESTION FURTHER. NOTICE WHAT BEGINS TO HAPPEN.

Defining Your Inner Landscape

I cannot say with confidence that this is a universal experience, although I suspect it may be, but upon asking myself that question I started to conjure up words that described my various roles and interests in life. I wrote down words like human, woman, daughter, wife, mother, friend, artist, musician and teacher. I thought of phrases that defined some of my interests: avid reader, loves cats. After a while my thought process came to a sudden halt. I heard myself saying, "Hey, wait a minute. You are so much more than the life roles that you fulfill. Dig deeper. Who are you, really?"

My mind began to sift through various descriptors of my physical characteristics and personality traits. White skin, big feet, generous, spiritual, kind, honest, joyous, afraid … I knew I had to keep going.

As I dug deeper still, statements about my values and beliefs began to emerge. What do I believe about my existence and purpose on Earth? What is important to me and why? What are my thoughts on family, faith, mortality, afterlife?

The inner landscape started to become very dense as I thought about my fears and shortcomings, my hopes and dreams. I watched the course of my life play itself out. I could see some of the daily experiences as well as the profound turning points that helped to shape me into the person that I am today. I thought about lessons I have learned through adversity, gifts I have received, and people who have made a difference in my life. I eventually reached a kind of epiphany—I realized that I am so much more than my body, my thoughts, my feelings and my experiences. I wrote a poem in an effort to capture this realization in words. I titled it "Pieces of Me" and it became the springboard for my self-portrait.

The following is a description of the creative process I experienced in designing my self-portrait. You may or may not choose to go this route; you should trust your instincts.

Holding a Personal Photo Session

Since I am primarily a mixed-media artist who loves to alter imagery, I decided to use a personal photograph as the basis for my work. I scheduled a personal photo session with Me, Myself and I. To capture my true self, I needed to do this on my own, without having to pose for someone else. I peered out a window at a beautiful snowscape, held my digital camera at arm's length, and began snapping away. Only one of the many photos I took seemed to capture my essence.

Altering the Image

As I studied the photo to see what it revealed about me, I decided to alter it to enhance as well as uncover some of my inner characteristics. I altered it both on the computer and by hand. I used Adobe Photoshop

Pieces of Me

Who am I? I am a wife, a mother, a daughter, an artist, a teacher, a musician, a friend, a student, and things that have not yet revealed themselves to me. I am more than my body, my thoughts, my experiences, my passions, and my fears. I am a work in progress. I am a divine soul; part of a greater tapestry of other divine souls —Beings of Light. I am here to evolve into my best self—to come to trust in the Universe, learn from adverse experiences, and revel in as much joy as I possibly can in this lifetime by being true to my soul.

Elements to digitally alter the style and saturation of the photograph. To make the image look less like a photograph and more like a painting, I chose the "rough pastel" feature and then intensified the saturation to a point where my face started to take on various hues of yellow, red, blue and pink. It was as if I could literally see the energies of my internal landscape blooming on my face.

I printed two copies of the altered image on inkjet photo paper. I cut one of the copies into random rectangles and squares, some of which I glued over the facial features on the other copy, giving it a "piecey" puzzle-like appearance. To emphasize the pieces, I outlined them with black colored pencil.

Choosing the Canvas

I was so excited to begin this part of the process. I wondered what was going to emerge. What would I learn about myself?

For my canvas I chose a 10" × 10" (25cm × 25cm) pre-primed stretched canvas. You should choose a substrate which resonates with you—perhaps a piece of wood, a vintage book cover or another found object.

In creating my self-portrait collage, I focused on four key elements: color, texture, text and personal embellishments (not necessarily in that order).

Selecting a Color Scheme

As I rummaged through my acrylics, I chose colors that spoke to me—colors that I thought represented the many facets of myself. In no time flat I had selected and grouped the armful of paints into families of yellow, blue, purple, red, pink, orange and ivory. Curiously, they were the same as the digital colors that had emerged in the altered photo.

Adding Texture

I glued some scraps of old sheet music to the canvas with a découpage medium. I purposely chose music to be the foundation of my portrait. Music has always been an important part of my life, and has been my saving grace more times than I care to mention. I coated the paper with watery yellow acrylic and blotted it with a paper towel to achieve a mottled effect. After it dried I added two more washes of leaf green and aqua, blending the colors together in some places.

Enhancing the Image With Text

I paged through my collection of vintage books in search of text that defined me. I cut out a handful of tiny words and instinctively glued them to my self-portrait's forehead. I dabbed at them with gesso to soften their edges and help blend them into the skin. I also added some

personal text that I did not want to share with others, then covered it up with layers of paint and gesso. Only I know where this text is and what it says.

Building More Texture

I absolutely love thick, dense textures, so I continued to build up my canvas, layer upon layer. As I did so, I realized that I was expressing the multiple layers of my own personal landscape—the intricacy of who I am as a person. I added more gesso, smeared on thick layers of oil pastel, added splashes of orange and purple acrylics, scribbled black colored pencil on parts of the canvas for depth, and glued down scraps of string and some additional scraps of sheet music.

I like to apply these mediums with my fingers, allowing me to feel more connected to the process—more natural, uninhibited and playful.

Listening to Your Inner Artistic Muse

Upon placing the altered photo on my created background, I realized that the two seemed too separate. My inner voice urged me to rip the altered image, to give it a choppier look. This was hard for me to do, because I was afraid of ruining all of the hard work I had put into the piece thus far. However, I chose to listen to my instincts. I took a deep breath and tore the image, trying to let go of my fears and trust in myself and the process. I accidentally scratched some of the pigment off while tearing—and to my pleasant surprise, it was serendipity at its best! I actually liked the effect, so I scratched a bit more. It was working! I was both excited and relieved. I adhered the pieces and blended gesso onto the edges to soften them and integrate them with the background.

Adding Personal Embellishments

This part is like the icing on the cake. I thought it was important to add a few embellishments that would symbolize elements of my life journey. I chose to use calendar scraps and highlighted them with gesso. They represent my daily experiences as well as the more profound turning points that have defined my life.

The broken paper heart is pieced back together with sheet music, representing the powerful role music has played in healing me, especially in my younger years. The purple string represents my life path; the color choice is indicative of the courage it takes to live each day authentically, being true to myself. The string travels up to the top of and, in my view, beyond the canvas, tethered to something much greater than myself.

The poem stands alone and hangs from a purple string beneath the canvas. I could not find a way to integrate it with the artwork without disrupting the flow of the piece. Instead, I mounted it on a background formed by a handful of pages torn from a book by George Eliot, a strong female author whom I admire and whose works have had an impact on my life.

used to be and who you may become. It is a way of finding and revealing your true self. It encompasses all of you—the good, the bad, the healthy, the injured and all of the gray matter in between.

Since we human beings are forever undergoing transformation, so should our art. I encourage you to revisit this powerful experience, as will I, to explore and document the changes within your personal landscape, all along celebrating every aspect of your being—all of the "pieces of you."

Reflecting on Your Portrait

It is my hope that you will create your own self-portrait, and that doing so will be an incredibly empowering learning experience for you as it has been for me, both as a human being and as an artist. Your self-portrait is a celebration of who you are at this moment, who you

UNLEASH YOUR INNER FRIDA
A Crown of Flowers

BY SUZANNE SIMANAITIS

If there's a patron saint of the alternative art scene, it's probably Frida Kahlo. Frida was laid up with horrific injuries and illnesses throughout her life, but she created a body of work that inspires us and left a personal history that fascinates us.

What I love about Frida is that she wasn't afraid to just be herself. She wore the traditional garments of her ancestral people despite the current fashions and depicted her stern unibrow even more prominently in self-portraits than it appeared in real life. Frida lived and loved with extreme passion, even confined to a hospital bed, where she hung a mirror and painted what she knew: the contours of her own face, the intricacy of her braided hair, the symbols of her rich inner story.

Many of Frida's paintings feature hearts, but not the valentine cartoon hearts we first imagine. No, Frida's heart is Frida's heart: exposed, damaged, suspended in time, arteries twining desperately toward some sturdy anchor they never found in her frail body. Some of Frida's paintings are downright gory in their depiction of her anatomical as well as her emotional truth. This woman was exploring her identity. She was asking questions and discovering ever-changing answers, and by gosh, she put it onto the canvas.

I wish I were more like Frida. Well, not the broken pelvis part. But I think you know what I mean. To get just a tiny bit closer to unleashing my inner Frida I created this crown of ribbon flowers, similar to the ones depicted in her *Self-Portrait Dedicated to Dr. Eloesser* and other paintings. Hey, growing a unibrow would be easier, but it would take longer. I am more of a tiara girl, anyway.

There are two main flower types in Frida's crown: roses and daisy-like flowers in a few colors and sizes. There are also some leaves and dangly little buds of unknown type. For the leaves and the dangly bits, use some of those gorgeous velvet leaves and berries you are hoarding for use in collage (this is what they were meant for!). We'll make the roses and daisy-like flowers. Let's start with a rose since it's the centerpiece. It's also incredibly easy!

Besides ribbon, needles, strong thread, scissors and a dime-store tiara to anchor it all, you'll need a small amount of crinoline, a stiff, open-weave material available at well-stocked fabric stores.

STARTING WITH THE ROSE

For the rose, choose 1½ yards (1.4 meters) of 1½"
(4cm) wide good-quality wired ribbon. I used ribbon
that is hot pink along one edge and pale yellow along
the other, and fashioned the rose so that the yellow
is buried deep within the flower, but a solid-colored
ribbon is fine to use.

1. Thread two or three needles, knot the thread ends and
   have these standing by. You'll be glad you did.

2. Lay one end of the ribbon on your workspace horizontally. Fold the end of the ribbon diagonally, as shown in
   Figure 1, so that the end is about 2½" (1cm) below the
   lower edge of the ribbon. I'll call this the "handle."

3. Take the triangle-shaped part you just folded down, and
   fold its leading edge back on itself as if beginning to roll
   up the ribbon (see Figure 2).

4. Holding the folded portion by the "handle" at the
   bottom, start to roll up the ribbon. Take care not
   to flatten or kink the top edge, which will form the
   graceful outer edges of the rose petals. Roll it two or
   three times around, and take a few small tucks at the
   bottom as you make each roll. The tucks will help the
   top edge of the ribbon to flare out a bit, giving the
   rose some lively form.

5. Stitch through the "handle" to attach the rose center
   to a 4" (10cm) square piece of crinoline.

6. At the other end of the ribbon, coax out the end of
   the wire that runs along the lower edge. Wrap the
   exposed wire around your scissors and gently pull the
   wire taut with one hand while you usher the ribbon
   along the wire with the other hand, gathering fullness
   into the ribbon the whole way down to where the
   rose center is stitched onto the crinoline.

7. Cut off the excess wire and discard it. Crimp the new
   end of the wire so that it does not slip back inside
   the ribbon.

8. Gently wrap the gathered ribbon around the rose
   center several times to create the appearance of wavy
   petals. Try to avoid a tightly wound bull's-eye; aim
   instead for a little fullness here, a little peekaboo
   there—just like the voluptuous beauty of a full-blown
   garden rose. Manipulate the edges of the gathered
   ribbon to form the rose to your liking, and place a
   few small stitches to secure it.

Voilà! That was much easier than you thought,
wasn't it? Once you learn to work with the ribbon the petals fall into place with only the slightest
encouragement from you.

CREATING THE REST OF THE BLOSSOMS

For each small four-petaled blossom (I made three
pink ones for the right side of the tiara and two
yellow ones for the left side,) cut a 10" (25cm)
length of 1" (3cm) wide wired ribbon. You will also
need something for the center of each flower, either
a small bunch of millinery flower stamens (which
you can find on eBay) or a petite button.

1. Fold the ribbon in half and then in half again,
   dividing the ribbon into four segments. Each segment
   will form a petal. (By increasing the length of the
   ribbon and adjusting the folding and stitching accordingly, you can create flowers with five or more petals.
   On my tiara, the two-tone orange flower consists of
   a five-petaled flower layered onto a seven-petaled
   one.)

2. Starting at one end of the ribbon, stitch a "U"-
   shaped pattern. At the top edge, when your needle

figure 1

figure 2

sort of stitches right off the ribbon, bring the next stitch around to the other side so that the thread wraps around the edge of the wired ribbon between each pair of petals (see Figure 3).

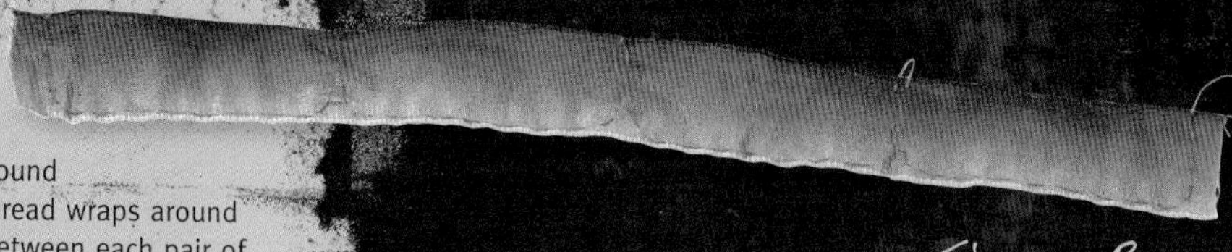

3. When you reach the end of the ribbon, gently gather it by holding the stitching thread taut and sliding the ribbon toward the knotted end. As you scrunch the ribbon, it will form four petals. Scrunch it firmly, as shown in Figure 4, and make a small stitch at the end of the gathered ribbon to secure the fullness. Then, to close the circle, make a tiny stitch next to the original anchor knot.

4. Tuck and trim the loose threads and ribbon edges to the back. Then make one stitch to secure the blossom onto a small piece of crinoline.

5. For the flower center:
   A. If you are using flower stamens, fold a few of them in half, tie them with some thread, and tuck the ends into the center of each flower. Make a few tiny stitches to anchor the stamens in place and draw the gathered center of each flower even more tightly closed around them. **B.** If you are using buttons for the flower centers, simply stitch one in the middle of each blossom.

6. Stitch the completed flowers of each type onto the same piece of crinoline. Each bloom will have its own internal logic about how the petals and stamens lay, so try to arrange them in a way that looks natural. Remember to group these little flowers together by color when you tack them onto scraps of crinoline, because that's the way Mother Nature does it in the garden. She is not a symmetrical or consistent kind of gal!

ASSEMBLING THE CROWN

To assemble your Frida floral crown, stitch, tie and wire the individual and grouped flowers onto a purchased plastic or wire tiara. It's OK to stitch through the bottom of a flower, as long as the stitches will be hidden in the voluptuous folds of the bloom.

WHEN YOU PERCH YOUR GLORIOUS CROWN ON YOUR HEAD, THINK OF FRIDA'S COURAGE, HER PASSION FOR LIFE AND ART AND, MOST OF ALL, THE HONESTY WITH WHICH SHE APPROACHED HER CREATIVE EXPRESSION. FEEL IT HUGGING YOUR HEAD AND USE THAT SENSATION AS A GENTLE REMINDER TO WORK TOWARD HER EXAMPLE.

figure 3

figure 4

The heart knows,
Listen to you, hear yourself.

The heart knows that existence is
not enough.
Pure joy is experienced
when the heart is fully
engaged in life.
Do not discount the power that
can come from within.

The heart
will sing
and dance, it
may even skip
a beat when
fully engaged.

The heart knows,
so listen quietly and
without waiting to
terribly long.
Hear what you heart
is saying. Understand,
that it may take
awhile.

The heart knows a little honesty
with yourself will also come in
handy. It may not
make senses at first
and that is to be
expected. So continue to
listen and nurture
the desire. Be true
to yourself and move forward
Sing the songs and dance the
dance that is your life.
Do not discount the power and
joy that can come from within.

LISTEN TO YOUR HEART

BY KATE LYON

i am your heart and i want you to know, something you may have forgotten ...i am singing the song the heartfue song that all hearts sing. it is a song of passion and desire. a desire for the love of life and if you follow me, your heart, I will lead you on a once in a life time journey. have trust and never doubt that i have your best interest within. Deep within we are one. So please listen to the songs that come from within and sing along.

do i listen; to be or not to be that is the question the hopes and dreams that I have locked away, do they dare to make their way to the surface, do i dare speak the words that come from the feelings locked away. only my heart holds the key. I hear it.

RANDI FEUERHELM-WATTS
SELF-PORTRAIT:

an artist bares all

Dear Suz,

It was so nice to hear from you after all this time. I have been so busy in art school and haven't had a chance to write. I've been working on a self-portrait zine. Why the interest in self-portraits, you ask? Who knows? I hate having my photo taken because I know that I am way cuter than that—I have to be. I just can't believe that the flab that appears in the photos is actually hanging around my face. It must be poor lighting, or that focus thing on my camera.

So here I am, trying to decipher my *Photography in Focus* book for the millionth time, and our professor assigns us this crummy self-portrait project. Great. Five months of self-portraits, and who in the world is going to be interested in looking at them, except maybe my mother? Page after page after page of me? Flabby-faced me? Maybe it's not too late to drop the class. I need to review chapter five on basic camera functions, and the instructor wants how many photos by Monday?

So that's how it all started. I wallowed through humiliating experiences like shooting a whole roll and then finding out the film didn't advance, setting the ISO wrong so all the photos came out black, and wasting even more film trying to figure out the timer thing so I could run over and get into the picture before it snapped. Then when I finally did get in front of the camera in time, what was I supposed to do? Stand there? Smile?

How many photos was I going to have of me smiling? Let's see: There's me smiling in front of the house. Me smiling with the dog. Me smiling while I am watering my plants. Smile. Smile. Smile. I look like I am auditioning for a toothpaste commercial. Obviously my teacher didn't buy this whole "Stepford wife" thing, so I was sent out to start all over again.

Searching through my photography textbooks for ideas, I found suggestions like, "Work of sight is done. Now do heart work on the pictures within you," and, "The material of the artist lies not within himself, nor in the fabrications in his imagination, but the world around him." My heart? My world?

In my Women in Art History class we learned that women painters in the late 1800s still couldn't portray themselves as painters. It was considered taboo for women to be artists, so when they painted self-portraits they had to be holding a hanky or doing needlepoint, while male artists were free to portray themselves holding palettes and staring intently at easels. Hmm. What to do? I didn't have a hanky or embroidery project handy, so what could I use for a prop?

What could I include in my photo that would represent the world around me?

I gazed out my window. Ashes. Black ashes. Black trees. Black ground. Black. Black. Black. We had just survived the wildfires that ravaged Claremont last autumn and since we live up in the middle of nowhere in a forested canyon—a formerly forested, now very black canyon, that is—it felt like we were the only ones left on Earth. No animals. No chirping birds or croaking toads, no crickets. So many trees were gone, you could see for miles now. And since no one was up here but me … I wondered … could I gather up all my nerve and take one nude photo outside? Just one? A photo of me and my environment, both stripped bare?

Now, Suz, you know that this is totally not my style. But for some strange reason I felt that I had to do it, and quickly, before I had time to change my mind. I slipped on a loose dress and flip-flops and went outside.

I positioned my camera on a tripod facing one of the few surviving but blackened trees by my house and set the timer. I had only eight seconds to run in front of the camera, pull the dress over my head, kick off my flip-flops and … now what do I do? Smile? "Click." My God, I did it. I can't believe I did it! That wasn't as hard as I thought it would be. Maybe I could take just one more, without the insipid smile this time. "Click." And another. "Click. Click. Click." I lay on logs, posed on rocks and grabbed onto large trees, and my feet got blacker and blacker from the ashes as I padded around the forest evaluating photo angles. Before I knew it, the whole roll of film was gone and I was hiking back up to the house to reload. I ended up spending half the day shooting photos in that deadened, silenced environment. I got so involved in what I was doing, I didn't even hear the truck coming up the road. Of all days, would you have guessed that the gas company guy would have picked today to come up to read the meter? My God!

Anyway, that was the beginning and the end of my nude modeling career. I still can't believe I did it and don't know if I will ever do it again. Please don't tell anyone; it's a little embarrassing.

From now on, appearing exclusively in photo booths at Kmart (fully dressed),

Randi

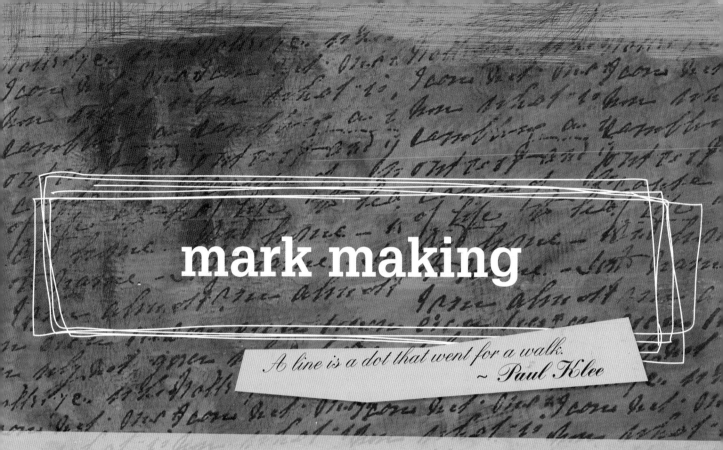

mark making

A line is a dot that went for a walk.
~ Paul Klee

Many of us (those of us who "can't draw") started our explorations in mixed-media art by picking up a rubber stamp. What a great solution—the image is drawn for us! Or maybe you are a scrapbooker, comfortable working with photos and recollections rendered in computer-generated fonts. From either starting place it's just a short hop to adding layers of interest via collage. But at some point, if you are being honest with yourself, you will feel compelled to pick up a tool and make a mark that is uniquely yours.

Although the results may seem discouraging at first, drawing is a skill worth acquiring. All you need is something to draw on, something to draw with, and patience.

Here is a secret: drawings do not have to look exactly like the objects they represent. If they did, where would the art be? The important thing is for each line to have a relationship with the next and with the edge of the page. Invent marks that express what you wish to communicate. Try many drawing implements and learn which ones respond most favorably to your movements.

Set aside your preconceived idea of "what it looks like" in favor of what is really there—what reveals itself when you are paying attention. That might mean sharp details or it might mean fleeting impressions.

There are, of course, other ways to make your mark.

Perhaps the most easily overlooked is your own handwriting. Oh, how I long to transform my regular, easygoing ("boring!") script into a jagged, expressive scrawl, or the curly-girly fanciful hand that comes naturally to others. I can, too, with practice. D'oh! There's that word again.

It's not necessary to invest hours practicing classic calligraphy. Examine your own normal writing and identify a key feature that you can develop. Maybe the descending tails of your letterforms are large loops—make them larger! Swoopier! Angular! Spirally! If your everyday handwriting combines uppercase and lowercase letters, or looks like a choppy ocean, all peaks and dips, exaggerate that tendency. Experiment with alternative mark-making tools like twigs and tracing wheels, and let the character of the tool determine the personality of your new letterforms.

Maybe your unique mark is meant to be a certain emotional logic in the use of colors or an energetic deconstruction of media previously laid down. Whatever kind of mark you choose to make, give yourself over to it on an instinctive level. Thinking gets in the way of mark making because we tend to think in words, and words carry meaning, and suddenly your mark turns into "a leaf" or "an eye." Let the marks be marks, and ignore the little voice inside your head that insists that leaves and eyes are pointed ovals, because sometimes they're not, and even when they are, they don't have to look that way in the version that you choose to communicate.

artwork at left:
PILAR POLLOCK, NICOLE LANDY, NIKKI BLACKWOOD

the Joy of Drawing

BY ELSIE SAMPSON

I was an artist until I turned thirteen. I was always carrying my little sketch pad around. I spent all my free time drawing. It made me happy. Then one day, I became a teenager. I became self-conscious about my "art" and thought, "I can't draw well, so I might as well not bother!" I know I was not alone. Don't we all know people who underestimate their creativity and insist that they can't draw?

Picasso once said, "All children are artists. The problem is how to remain an artist once he grows up." Maybe many of us grew up too soon.

I didn't start sketching regularly again until I was nearly thirty years old. Sure, I still can't draw like Leonardo da Vinci, but I once again carry my sketchbook everywhere I go, and the joy of drawing is back! I especially like to sketch while visiting friends or when I go out to eat. I sketch the furniture, the food I eat, the views I see while traveling by train to New York City, the mess I made in my kitchen and even the street corner where my car stopped for a long traffic light. Any bits and pieces of my life are my still-life setup for practicing drawing.

I journal these bits and pieces of daily life according to my mood of the day, and have developed different drawing styles. I wonder, if someone had told me that I didn't need to take college-level drawing classes in order to draw but I could just play and have fun on my sketch pads, would I have started journaling with sketching sooner?

I wanted to share with everyone the fun I experience from carefree drawing, and so I created a few zines that are completely hand-drawn/written, including *Chinese Sketchbook*. I was thrilled to hear from my readers that they feel inspired to pick up a pencil again after a long time or "tickled" to draw lightheartedly. Some show me pictures of what they sketched, and some tell me that they would now sketch even banana peels! It reminds me of the joy of sketching I felt when I was a child.

Sketching at ...

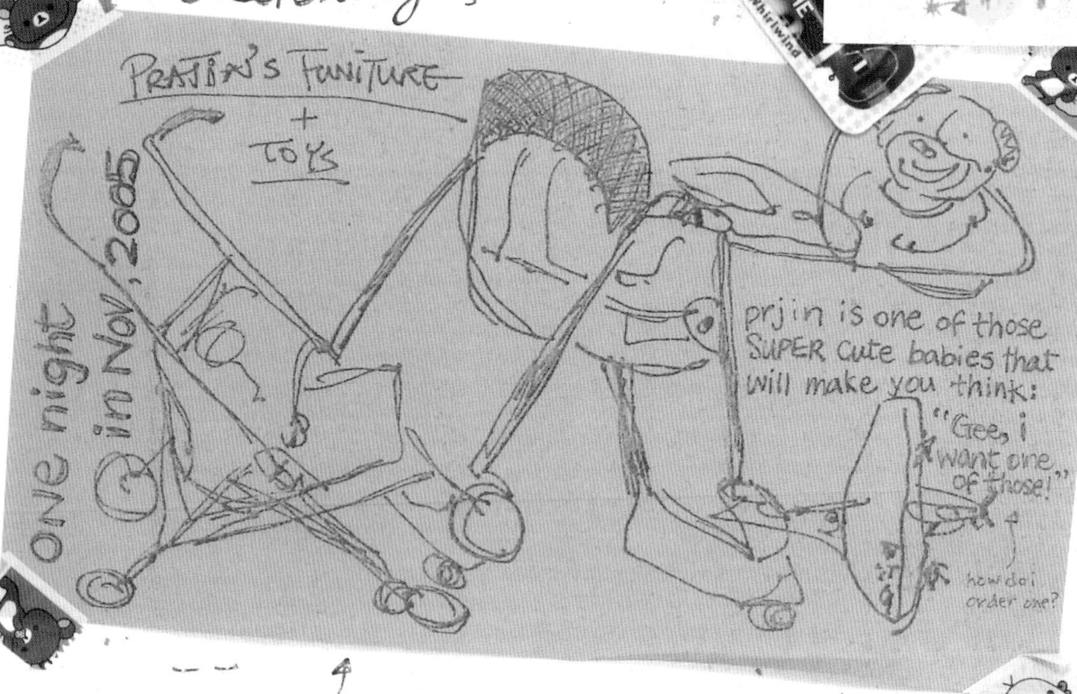

PRAJIN'S FURNITURE + TOYS

one night @ in Nov, 2005

prjin is one of those SUPER cute babies that will make you think:

"Gee, i want one of those!"

how do i order one?

my friend's house

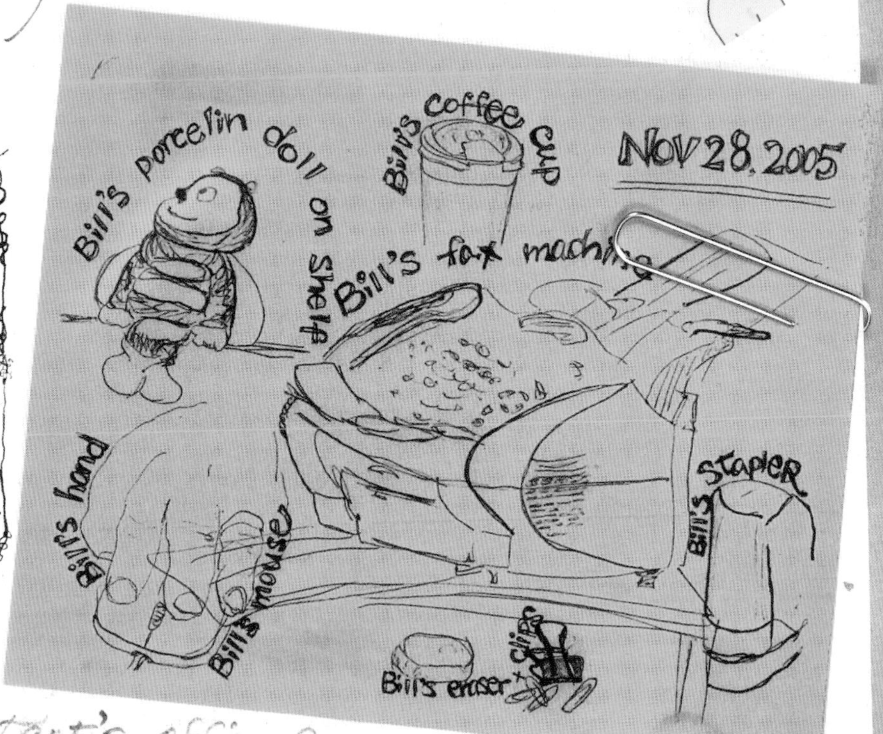

Sketch on Scraps!

The above sketch was done on one of those index cards comes with photo storage boxes and Sharpie.

The one on this page was a piece of yellow scrap and very crappy green ball pen!

Bill's porcelin doll on shelf

Bill's coffee cup

NOV 28, 2005

Bill's fax machine

Bill's hand

Bill's mouse

Bill's eraser + clips

Bill's stapler

accountant's office

HERE ARE SOME TIPS THAT MAY HELP MAXIMIZE YOUR ENJOYMENT OF SKETCHING/DRAWING:

- ▷ Make it a habit to sketch every day, even just for a minute.
- ▷ Don't worry about the outcome—enjoy the process.
- ▷ Draw what's near you: your hands, your wallet, your shoes . . .
- ▷ Draw regular objects from unusual angles. This can train your hands to capture what you really see instead of what your brain thinks things should look like.
- ▷ Adding color to sketches brings images to life.
- ▷ Drawings don't have to be completed.
- ▷ You don't need the best tools on earth to draw; good drawings may happen on scrap papers or even restaurant napkins.
- ▷ Draw what pleases your *EYES*: your pets, candy, favorite shirts . . .
- ▷ Try drawing with simple lines.
- ▷ Draw things upside down. (It's up to you whether to set your still-life upside down or position yourself upside down—both ways will be fun!)
- ▷ Try different pens and drawing surfaces.
- ▷ Keep your hands moving and capture the moments.
- ▷ Try to draw an object with one continuous line.
- ▷ You don't have to show your sketchbook to anybody if you don't want to.

When I sketch in public places, conversations arise between me and strangers that would never have happened under normal circumstances. I met a musician who, to earn money, wears an advertising "sandwich board" on a street corner; he offered to pose for me since his job is to stand there anyway. I met a mother of four who used to sculpt before she was married, and a street vendor who offered me a free bottle of water because I sketched him and his booth. It took me a while to get used to the occasional attention from strangers, but I do love the positive energy generated by sharing what I enjoy doing. It also helps me to realize that I don't have to be the best to be an artist!

VINTAGE LABELS

I LOVE THESE LABELS. THEY ARE NOT CHEAP BUT BEAUTIFUL. TAKA WAS THINKING ABOUT MY ZINES WHEN SHE BOUGHT THIS BOX SET SO I'M GOING TO HONOR HER THOUGHTS AND INCLUDE 1 LABELS IN EACH COPY OF THE ARTIST EDITION.

▷ TAKA 村

SHE KNOWS WHAT HER FRIEND WANTS!

the apron is not sketched, it's my poor drawing!

♥ A BEAUTIFUL DESIGNER APRON! WHO ELSE OULD THINK OF GETTING ME AN APRON? LOVE IT!

i GUESS SOMEBODY READ "RECALLING MY CHILDHOOD MEMORY" FROM CHINESE SWEATSHOP 1!

HELLO KITTY stickers, pencil and note pad.

THIS IS A VERY COOL RECIPE BOOK. A LOT OF CUTE PICTURES. HEALTHY RECIPES FOR CANINES AND INTERESTING QUOTES X BY COOPER GILLESPIE & SALLY SAMSON ISBN 0-7432-5591-7(1103)

THROW ME A BONE

OK, Emily! SHE MADE ME A VERY DELICIOUS COCONUT PASSION FRUIT CAKE AND BROUGHT IT ALL THE WAY FROM BROOKYN TO ARDESLY, WESTCHESTER IT JUST WARMS MY ♡ TO KNOW THAT SOMEONE IS WILLING TO GO THROUGH THIS KIND OF TROUBLE FOR . . . MY BIRTHDAY !!

very beautiful chocolate hand writing

Happy Birthday Elsie

mango slices

Shopping is fun!

OLD NAVY

FROM TUNDE/ARAP

IF YOU HAVE READ "Shopping Queen's Diary", YOU'LL KNOW HOW i feel about shopping. TUNDE AND ARAP GOT ME A GIFT CARD TO SHOP! HE HE! NOW YOU KNOW WHERE DO i NEED TO GO AFTER i'm DONE FOR THESE FEW PAGES! ♡

DARSHANA ONLY STARTED TO BEAD THIS SUMMER. SHE MADE ME THIS SWEET LITTLE BRACELET WITH GLASS BEADS. VERY NICE SELECTION OF BEADS. YOU GO GIRL!

more great presents! i received from friends and family were not included cos' these pages are from my diary about the birthday party! ♡

FINDING FACES

BY CARLA SONHEIM

I see faces—in sidewalk cracks, tree branches, soap scum, light reflections, fur markings, pancake bubbles and abstract paintings.

When I was about ten years old, "scribble drawing" was a favorite pastime. I would scribble something, then I would "finish" the drawing I had "started." (There is one drawing I still remember—I kept it for years—that is one of the most expressive things I've ever done. It was a little guy playing a guitar, something I never would have thought to draw. He just presented himself to me.)

The creatures you see here are products of the same impulse. I use gel medium to glue down scraps of torn sewing patterns to watercolor paper in random shapes. I usually do ten at a time, just slapping them down with no thought as to outcome, encouraging wrinkles and texture. By the time I finish gluing down the tenth scrappy shape, the first one is dry enough to "finish." I use a Micron .01 black pen to draw eyes, claws, etc. Sometimes I add color with acrylic paint.

The creatures aren't always immediately apparent. I turn the paper around and around until I see it. Something always comes eventually—it never fails.

I approach painting the same way. For years I didn't consider myself an "artist" because I couldn't see things in my head before I drew them. When I took my first painting class, I was one of the few people who didn't know ahead of time what I was going to paint. Luckily I had a teacher who encouraged this approach. Now, when faced with blank canvases, I just put brush to canvas and start moving the paint around. Within a minute or two (or sometimes more), an animal or face emerges. Then I simply finish what I've found.

I encourage you to let yourself be surprised by your art. Try making a handful of "scribble drawings." Just doodle patterns and shapes, then look at what is there to be discovered, or start a painting with no thought as to the outcome. It's a wonderfully freeing way to create.

arting and crafting with metal

BY NICOLE LANDY

Learning to handcraft metal items from lightweight sheet metal opens up a world of creative possibilities. The technique is simple, the tools basic—you probably have most of them already. This process holds promise for card makers, scrapbookers, altered book artists and journalers, as well as collage and assemblage artists. With just a little imagination you will reap great rewards, and you'll find that amazing results belie the small effort that's expended.

metal picture frames

These frames are fabulous to display family photos or art. Smaller versions look beautiful on the front of a card.

what to do

1. Cut the image you wish to frame into the desired shape--square, rectangular, round or oval. You may want to use a template for this.

2. Working on an embossing mat, place the image on the reverse side of the metal sheet using gum putty to temporarily secure it. Make sure that the piece of metal is large enough to execute the design you want. You will be working on the reverse side because you want the relief, rather than the indentation, to appear on the right side of the frame.

3. Use a stylus to trace around the image and emboss the cutout shape onto the metal. Use a ruler or template to steady your hand, if necessary. Remove the image and set it aside.

4. Now you are ready to create an attractive frame shape, as well as to fill in that shape with ornamental patterns. Use ink pads and rubber stamps to imprint a shape and patterns, or draw your own with a permanent marker.

5. Emboss the shape and patterns with embossing tools, creating lines, repetitive patterns, dots of various sizes, squiggles, hearts and so forth, using light to moderate pressure with the tools. When you are satisfied with the design, flip the metal over.

6. Carefully cut along the outer edge of the frame shape.

7. To reinforce the thin, delicate metal, make a backing for the frame by placing it on a piece of mat board and tracing around it with a pencil. Use a craft knife and cutting mat to cut the mat board just inside the traced line so that it is slightly smaller than the metal shape. (This can also be done using heavy-duty

what you'll need

- photo or artwork to frame
- scissors
- embossing mat
  A FIRM BUT YIELDING SURFACE, SUCH AS A MOUSEPAD OR THE PAGES OF A PHONE BOOK
- light- or medium-weight sheet metal
  (36–38 GAUGE), ANY COLOR
- gum putty
  FOR TEMPORARILY ADHERING PHOTO AND EMBELLISHMENTS
- embossing tools (see tip on page 38)
- metal ruler
- Dover catalogs of ornamental designs
  OR ANY OTHER INSPIRATIONAL SOURCES TO HELP YOU CREATE ATTRACTIVE SHAPES AND PATTERNS
- black pigment ink pad and rubber stamps
- fine-point permanent marker
- mat board
- pencil
- craft knife
- flat paintbrush or a stippling brush
- acrylic paint in tubes
  DARK COLORS LIKE BURNT UMBER AND RAW UMBER ARE MOST EFFECTIVE
- heavy gel medium or E-6000 glue
- paper towel
- rubbing alcohol
- cotton swabs
- embellishments
  GLITTER GLUE, METALLIC RUB-ONS, RHINE-STONES, BEADS, BUTTONS, CHARMS, JUNK JEWELRY AND SO ON
- jewelry glue
- picture-hanging hardware
- sunglasses
  NO KIDDING!—THE LIGHT GLINTING OFF THE METAL CAN BE QUITE BLINDING AT TIMES

metal collage elements

Whatever it is that you like to use as collage or assemblage embellishments, chances are good that you can make it in metal. In addition to design elements and images, you can emboss whole phrases or single words using steel letter punches on the front side of the metal, so this lettering will be impressed into the metal, not raised. Or try your hand at freestyle script, using an old ballpoint pen on the front side, or if you want the writing to be raised, you can "write" the words backwards onto the back of the metal.

Try making photo corners, as simple or as elaborate as you like—they are so easy to execute. Trim decorative borders with fancy-edged scissors to embellish anything and everything.

The beauty of these hand-tooled elements is that they are lightweight and relatively flat, so they're ideal for cards, scrapbooks, journals and altered books, as well as for collage and assemblage artworks. With this simple technique, you can customize elements to complement any theme. You need not lament an embellishment you wish you had—make it yourself, and make it your own!

scissors.) Paint the mat board to match the metal, for a finished look.

8. Adhere the frame to the backing with heavy gel medium or epoxy. Press gently together, being careful not to mar or flatten the embossed pattern.

9. I like to tone down and antique the metal with burnt umber paint for a warm effect or raw umber paint for a cool effect. Using a dry paintbrush, apply undiluted paint from the tube, making sure to work it into all the nooks and crannies. Lightly graze the surface with a damp cloth or paper towel to remove the paint from the raised areas, without removing the paint that collects in the grooves. This will create a beautiful patina with shiny and matte areas and contrasting lights and darks. If the paint dries too quickly, use rubbing alcohol on a paper towel or cotton swab to remove it.

10. When the paint is dry, use gel medium to glue the image onto the frame, in the reserved space.

11. Next, have fun with embellishments: glitter glue, metallic rub-ons, rhinestones and so on. Echo the colors in your photo for harmony.

12. When everything is completely dry and all embellishments are securely adhered, glue picture-hanging hardware on the back. The frame is so light that nails are not needed.

additional supplies for further inspiration

- Tracing paper or carbon paper
- Punching and piercing tools
  STEEL LETTER AND NUMBER PUNCHES, LEATHER TOOLING PUNCHES, SCREWDRIVER BITS, NAIL HEADS OR SCREW HEADS
- Small hammer
  TO USE WITH THE PUNCHES
- Cookie cutters
- Metal stencils of patterns and images
- Rubber stamps
- Glass paint and colored permanent markers

Source of inspiration for design of frecian picture frame. From a collage/scrapping project.

what to do

Always working on the reverse side of the metal sheet, there are several different ways to create elements, designs and patterns.

1. Draw an image onto the metal freehand using a permanent marker, trace an image with tracing or carbon paper and transfer it to the metal with a stylus, use a rubber stamp and pigment ink to stamp the design onto the metal, or place an object on the metal and trace around it with a marker.

2. Once the design is on the metal, place the metal on your embossing mat, reverse (or marked) side up, and use a stylus to outline the shape. Emboss details, designs and patterns with various embossing tools (see Embossing Tools, this page). If you want dimensional relief over a large surface, use the smooth rounded end of a large paintbrush. Look in the kitchen, the garage and the junk drawer and marry your imagination with all the impromptu tools at hand to achieve your goal—anything goes.

3. When you are satisfied with how it looks on the front side, carefully cut around the embossed image with scissors. If you want to cut out any holes or shapes with a punch, do so now. To remove bits like the hole in a keyhole, punch a starter hole and finish the job with small, sharp detail scissors.

4. Antique the finished element as described in step 9 on page 37.

Voilà! It couldn't be simpler. The hardest part will be stopping yourself from creating metal facsimiles of everything under the sun, including the sun and the moon. . . and the stars. . .

a few more ideas...

- Try adding white acrylic to colored paint, to opaque it, and then brush it on the metal for a beautiful whitewash effect.
- Try embossing on both sides of the metal, for an interesting mix of concave and convex markings.
- Extremely small or very dimensional pieces can be made stronger by filling the embossed areas with wood putty or air-dry clay.

embossing tools

Almost any pointed or round-tipped object can be used as an embossing tool. A double-ended embossing stylus has large and small heads for broad and fine indentations. If you don't have a stylus, a dried-out ballpoint pen will get the job done. A dressmaker's tracing wheel or a pastry wheel will indent perfectly-spaced dotted lines. A scalloped pastry edger is also useful.

DRAWING THE WHITE RABBIT

by Pilar Isabel Pollock

The first time I read Lewis Carroll's *Alice's Adventures in Wonderland*, I was nine years old. Before that, I knew the story through Disney cartoons and listening to the librarian read the work out loud to my class on Tuesday afternoons during my second grade year. Yes, I knew who Alice was, but I did not know Alice.

When I was nine years old and in fourth grade, my teacher dispatched a five-member squad to the school library every twenty minutes like clockwork (going in alphabetical order). We were to find a title to read during those minutes of dead time when we had completed an assignment early or when the teacher went into the hall to talk to the principal. Since Fate had granted me a surname starting with "P" I was in the final group of kids to visit the library, and the new releases and popular books inevitably had been claimed by the time it was my turn. So I spent my twenty minutes exploring the stacks for a title that would speak to me.

It was on one of my treasure hunts in the stacks that dear Alice appeared. I remember the faded cover was muted, the upper right corner of the book was frayed, and the pages had a peppery musk from shelf wear and time. I can explain my delight at the weight of the book in my bag, the joyful crinkle of the protective book cover under my little hands or the awe I felt when the book opened to the exact page where I had left off. I don't know if I can explain the magic which occurs when one opens a book that is destined to become a lifelong friend: the sudden click of an internal door when the right key has been found, or the warm wash of a hidden knowledge emerging from the recesses of the mind when the book whispers secrets which you have long suspected.

There is a phase in each person's life when one is not quite a child but not yet a young adult. It is as if one wakes up in the morning and suddenly the world has changed into a strange and curious place—a realm where the rules have changed and everything you believed to be true is no longer relevant. Perhaps the most dramatic example of this shift occurs at school: creative play and exercises used to teach "the three Rs" are replaced by rigid timetables and sentence diagrams; social hierarchies begin to develop in the classroom, as well as on the playground; one is told one must color within the lines, and free-form, abstract coloring is silenced by expectations of more "realistic" drawings.

In fourth grade, this confining new world was a world I

Alice continued to teach me this lesson. A few months after I first read *Wonderland*, I found this lesson manifest both figuratively and literally. Perhaps it was coincidence, but during art class we were assigned to draw a picture of the White Rabbit in his herald outfit. Our art instructor was the parent of a student in the school, who volunteered her time teaching art to each grade. For each session, she would place a picture of an object on the overhead projector and we were to draw a carbon copy of the object on our construction paper. We received very little instruction as the art "teacher" often sat behind the desk reading a magazine. Our pictures were graded based on our ability to create a likeness to the object, and the margin for error was nonexistent. My previous pictures had received failing grades for my inability to create a passing likeness. I hoped the White Rabbit would bring me luck and I would finally earn a decent grade.

Unfortunately, my paper ended up filled with eraser marks. In the middle of this mess was my interpretation of the rabbit: his head was too long, his ears too short and I will not mention how his body looked like a colorful bunch of sticks. Obviously, my White Rabbit was not going to pass, and upon receiving another failing grade my eyes welled with tears.

Realizing how upset I was, my fourth grade teacher asked me to stay after class. Ms. Stevens looked at my rabbit and complimented me on my use of color and my attempts to shade the poor lopsided creature. I suspect she knew how hard I had tried to capture the exact form of the White Rabbit in his herald outfit. She had witnessed the extra time I'd spent examining the original drawing and she had recorded my previous art scores in her grade book. She had seen my face grow red with frustration and my eyes fill with heartbreak during each art class as I desperately attempted the assignments.

An accomplished artist herself, Ms. Stevens called me over to her desk and picked up a copy of the picture the art "teacher" had used for our prompt. She

strived to understand. While you may think a nine-year-old could not fully appreciate the complexity of *Wonderland*, my own nine-year-old mind clearly realized Carroll had whispered the secrets of adulthood within the story's text: you may not *create Wonderland*, but you have the power to define it.

asked me to watch as she took a red pen and circled the rabbit's ears, his head, his trumpet, and the various details of his outfit. On the side of the rabbit, Ms. Stevens drew a circle, a square, a triangle, an oval and a line. She then asked me to look at the picture of the rabbit and tell her what she had marked in pen. Within the red parameters, the

rabbit's ears were no longer ears, but long ovals with pointy ends; his face looked like a triangle that turned into a circle. Suddenly, I realized the rabbit was made up of a series of shapes. With my chubby black pencil, I began to follow Ms. Stevens' lead and draw each shape until they made up the whole rabbit.

That day I learned the fundamentals of drawing and began to understand the power of one's perception in the creation of one's world.

In the final chapter of *Alice's Adventures in Wonderland*, Alice is liberated from the constructs of the neurosis of Wonderland when she asserts and chooses her own perspective: "Who cares for you? . . . You are just a pack of cards." Through this pronouncement, Alice strips away the layers of Wonderland's chaos and confusion to reveal the very essence of her oppressors. As artists, there are times when we will become bound by an idea and an expectation of how our process and creations should manifest. We will experience frustration and artistic blockage until we cannot create, but only worry. I think back to my ninth year and my epiphany that, like Alice, I could reclaim my power by understanding the world was not what it appeared to be and it was my choice to decide how I wanted to see it. I think about how Ms. Stevens revealed to me that I could draw if I changed the way I saw the rabbit. There are times in creative life when we need to adjust our view in order to see what truly obstructs our ability to create. In doing so, we identify what is real and what is not, thus reclaiming power. We can honor and learn from our experiences in Wonderland, but we must remember that we have the power to define and shape our art and our lives.

MAIL ART TO THE SELF
BUILDING A POSTCARD BOOK

BY Juliana Coles ART BY Nikki Blackwood

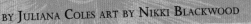

This is a fun, fast-paced and exciting introduction to my Expressive Visual Journaling® process that takes the fear out of self-expression by disguising it as a cool mail art project. On the following pages we'll create a journal, and, later in the Imagination chapter, I'll walk you through a unique journaling process for self-discovery—and you'll begin a dialogue that may turn out to be a joyous, lifelong pursuit.

PHASE 1: GATHER YOUR SUPPLIES
Collect all your tools and materials before you begin creating. Everything must be ready at arm's length, so that you can work spontaneously. You do not want to have to think; you will not have time to search.

warning: If you have not completely set up your work area with your tools and materials, stop here. Do not read further. Do not read ahead to get an idea of what's next. It is important that you do not know what comes next. So stop right now, go to the store to get what you need, and set up your workspace.

SUPPLIES

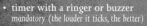

- **timer with a ringer or buzzer**
  mandatory (the louder it ticks, the better)
- **cardboard or mat board**
  you'll need plenty of it (four or five big pieces) but nearly anything will do: corrugated box panels, mat board, the backs of legal pads—different sizes, thicknesses and textures will only add to the uniqueness of your project
- **paintbrushes, various sizes**
- **acrylic paints**
  any kind, any colors (at least one light and one dark)
- **brush-tip markers** *(at least two colors)*
- **black permanent marker**
- **rags or paper towels**
- **other favorite art materials**
  you'll know which elements will make your work yours. (Include wet and dry media)
- **glue stick**
- **collage stuff**
  photographs, cancelled and faux postage, handwritten letters, photocopies of anything precious, book full of good words standing by to be cut up
- **pencil**
  if you can get a 6B artist pencil or a graphite stick (not charcoal) you will be able to write juicier
- **scissors**
- **rubber stamp alphabet and numbers**
- **other rubber stamps that you love**
  patterns, textures, postal cancellations, text
- **permanent ink pad(s)**
  I like StazOn because the ink dries quickly and works on slick surfaces
- **jar of water**
- **ruler**
- **masking tape**
- **clear packing tape**
- **other kinds of tape, plain and fancy**
  I love tape
- **binder rings**
  1" or 1½" (3cm or 4cm), two of them
- **eyelets**
  ¼" (6mm), tools to set them and a firm surface to work on (like a mini anvil or a kitchen cutting board)

PHASE 2: CREATE YOUR BACKGROUNDS

You're going to create background texture on these boards—problems to solve later. So, no picture making or trying to impress your imagined audience. Just follow the instructions and create backgrounds.

Remember, you are on a need-to-know basis only. Do not read ahead. Read each numbered step, set the timer for the allotted period, and perform the step before you read further.

If you're not done in the given amount of time, stretch yourself by moving on anyway. Don't say to yourself, oh, *five more minutes and this will look great.* Don't care how it looks. Get mad, get over it—move on. If you're frustrated, you're right on track.

Be like a scientist, not an artist. This is just research. You want to see what happens when you layer different things. You should be quite happy if these panels are a complete mess when you're done. Extreme Visual Journalists push the parameters of all we know. We want to get to the other side; we seek that which is unknown. We don't have time to worry about making "art." We are after something meatier. As a matter of fact, we should feel successful if these panels don't turn out like we'd hoped and they make us uncomfortable. We want to stretch ourselves by releasing our attachment to the outcome. We will work very quickly and use as many mediums as possible, letting go of all desire to make a "nice" or "good" picture. Instead we'll learn something we never knew and allow ourselves to enjoy the exploration.

In the following process you will be working on four or five pieces of cardboard or mat board. Each piece has two sides. When the instructions say "paint three boards," I mean any three sides among all the boards. You could do the front and back of one board plus one side of another board, or one side on three different boards. It is important to work all boards at the same time, so let some dry while you work on others. *Do not make a picture. Make a mess.* Do not worry about filling each space completely and do not worry about leaving space for what comes next: You *do not know* what comes next. Uncertain? Good. Feeling rushed and unprepared? You've got it now. Keep going, especially if you feel resistance—just try it, even if it goes against every fiber of your being. Don't worry about the outcome; stay focused on the process. If you finish the exercise before the timer buzzes, keep going, either with the same board or another. Never stop.

1. Completely cover three sides with paint. Set your timer for five minutes, and **GO!** Do not make a painting. Do quick coverage. Don't use that little brush, grab a big one—better yet, use a brayer or a wad of paper or your hand. Time will be up quickly.

2. Now add some writing to all of the boards. You can write on painted sides or blank sides—just remember that in the end, all sides need to have something on them. You have five minutes; set the timer. Use a brush-tipped marker, and get over it. You can wipe the paint with a rag to dry it off first. If the marker doesn't work, it doesn't matter. Just keep writing. List all the places you long to travel. Write as large as you can. Larger! And write in cursive. If you write big and fast, you may have to write over some of your previous writing in order to keep going, but don't stop until the timer dings.

3. Randomly grab fifteen magazine clippings or photographs—any kind of shiny or glossy paper. You don't have time to plan; just rip, tear or cut and glue down. Place five images on each of three boards; you have ten minutes. This is where a quick-drying glue stick comes in handy. Just grab and glue. Don't care what it is, don't care what it looks like, just go, go, go.

4. Select fifteen non-glossy, paper collage items (book pages, newspaper bits or photocopies). Adhere five of them to each of three sides in ten minutes. Set the timer.

5. Next, print a repeating pattern. Do not use rubber stamps or ink pads for this step. Pour out a little paint and find something to print with—an eraser, the cap of a paint bottle—something within arm's reach, something that makes a specific shape, not something fluffy like a sponge that can change its form every time. Be selective about where you put this pattern. Try at least three different patterns on three different sides. You have five minutes. Make sure at this point that almost all sides of all your boards have something on them. Grab one that has little or nothing on it and go.

6. Add some marks with a graphite pencil. Hold it like a little kid (in a fist) or with your non-dominant hand—no control. Just doodle around: thick lines, thin lines, squiggly lines, how dark can you go, how light? Outline some of the stuff that's already there. Do not try to draw a picture. Make marks on two different boards in five minutes.

7. Take five minutes to randomly cut out words, sentences and phrases that appeal to you from magazines or books. Don't glue them down, just collect.

8. Create found poetry using only the words you just cut out (don't cut out more to try to make it better.) You don't have to use all your words. Glue the poetry onto

a board. Words can go around the edges or right across the center or they can zigzag. You have ten minutes.

9. On any three boards create a pattern, but this time with rubber stamps and ink pads. Don't put the pattern everywhere—a little here, a little there. Don't neglect the edges of the boards. Five minutes.

10. Now paint three more sides. If there is stuff already on it, paint right over it. Use a rag to wipe off some of the paint, exposing the images. Experiment with rubbing paint in and rubbing paint off; feel free to add a little water. Do not "save" anything. Paint over the whole thing. Even if you love it, paint over it. Work spontaneously and without attachment.

11. Finally, look at all sides of all the boards. If there are vast areas of emptiness, add some paint or an image or a pattern here and there. Cardboard showing through is fine, just not super-large gaps. Make sure that each board has at least one thing going off the edge. Set the timer for fifteen minutes and quickly touch up the empty areas on all boards. Still no picture making, just texture.

PHASE 3: CREATE YOUR POSTCARDS

Cut the boards into postcard pieces measuring 5" x 7" (13cm x 18cm). Let's play "Operation" with the leftover scraps: piece them together into new boards, Frankenstein-style. This is my favorite step—I love the wounded things. They are so much more interesting and vital. Nothing is ever a loss because everything is recyclable and has a purpose and a fit.

Lay two scraps side by side with the bottom edges flush. Use a piece of masking tape to create a suture, taping the two scraps together. Turn the piece over and add another strip of tape to the back. Wrap a long strip of masking tape the whole way around the seam. Keep adding tape until the "wound" feels strong. Now line up another scrap and bind it onto the growing piece. Keep taping together cardboard scraps until you have a panel that can be cut down to make more 5" x 7" (13cm x 18cm) postcards. Wrap the edges with more tape to unify each pieced postcard.

PHASE 4: BUILD YOUR JOURNAL

Pick seven cards for your postcard book (five pages and two covers). Choose the ones that have the most meat to work with, the ones that are saying, "Me! Pick me!" You will know.

(The rest of your postcards are Mail Art. Add a To/From label, more collage stuff if you want to, lots of postage and—voilà! How easy and fun was that? Now mail one to yourself, one to me and one to your best friend.)

The pages of your journal will be held together with binder rings slipped through eyelets set into the boards. For ¼" (6mm) eyelets, a ³⁄₁₆" (5mm) hole works best. Punch two holes along the spine edge of one postcard page, ½" (1cm) from the spine edge and 1" (3cm) from the top and the bottom edges (see photos). Go ahead and use a ruler to measure the hole placement on the first page, and then use this postcard as a template to mark and

punch the holes in the other six pages so they will line up.

In each hole, set an eyelet. Don't be ladylike. Put some elbow into it. Place an eyelet into a hole, set the piece on a firm surface, hold the eyelet-setting tool straight up and down with the tip resting in the back end of the eyelet, and hammer it home. Don't worry about getting them right—they'll look great. Me? I always pound them vigorously at the end to make them all flat and weird shaped.

To assemble, stack the postcards in the order you want them, with the "covers" on the outside and all the eyelets along the left side. Open the binder rings and slip them through the holes to form your book. Snap the rings firmly shut.

Congratulations! You are done with the book form and ready for your next taste of Expressive Visual Journaling. Meet me on page 82 for the journaling exercises!

LETTERING
for the non-calligrapher
BY PATTI MONROE-MOHRENWEISER

Words can be an interesting way to add emotion, express ideas and even add texture. Yet many people are reluctant to use their own lettering because they aren't "calligraphers." While calligraphic skill has its benefits, there are lots of things that you can do with letters and straightforward writing to add a new dimension to your artwork.

Marks and letters can be made with a huge variety of implements. Very early on in my calligraphic training, a teacher had us bring in items from home to use as writing tools—the more challenging, the better. Along with sticks and nails and silverware, my favorite contribution was a pink disposable razor! The range of letters from these simple tools was amazing; I was hooked!

Getting the thicks and thins, textures and variations in your lettering is much easier than you think. Many useful tools are probably on your art table right now. These tools can add a totally new look to your artwork.

CARPENTER'S PENCILS

Available at your local hardware store, these wide lead pencils can be turned on their side for a loose monoline style (Figure 1, p.48), or used with the broad edge for chunky letters (Figure 2, p.48). Imagine that you only had one or two words to fill up an entire line. Really stretch those letters across your page (Figure 3, p.48)!

POPSICLE STICKS

First, cut the rounded end off to square it up, and use a craft knife to bevel the end slightly (so it isn't as thick). Dip your new tool into some watered-down ink or watercolor, and you will get some wonderful, organic letterforms (Figure 4, p48). Try uppercase letters; try lowercase letters. Don't limit yourself!

CHOPSTICKS

The inexpensive wooden ones (available free at your local Chinese takeout) can be used "as is" or sharpened into various sized points. Dip them into ink and try some loose, random lettering (Figure 5, p.48).

MAT BOARD

Cut scraps about 4" (10cm) long, and in widths of ½" (1cm), ¾" (2cm) and 1" (3cm) for some inexpensive, throwaway tools. Dip them into watered-down acrylic paint, watercolor paint or ink, and try some extra large letters (Figure 6, p.48). Cutting some notches into the ends of the mat board will result in "double-stroked" or "scroll" letters (Figure 7, p.48).

In addition to these tools, there are other art supplies that will further enhance the layered-letter effect:

ART MASKING FLUID

Used to protect or "mask" areas of the paper, this fluid makes these areas resistant to watercolor and other media. Tinted masking fluid is the easiest to see on white paper, so adding a drop or two of watercolor to the bottle of fluid can be very helpful. Using a brush or other implement, write letters on watercolor paper, using masking fluid. When the fluid is dry, paint over it with watercolors or fluid acrylics. When your painting is dry, remove the masking fluid with a rubber cement pickup, or rub it off gently with your fingers. Make sure to test the masking fluid on your chosen paper first. Some papers are not compatible, and will tear or lift when the fluid is removed.

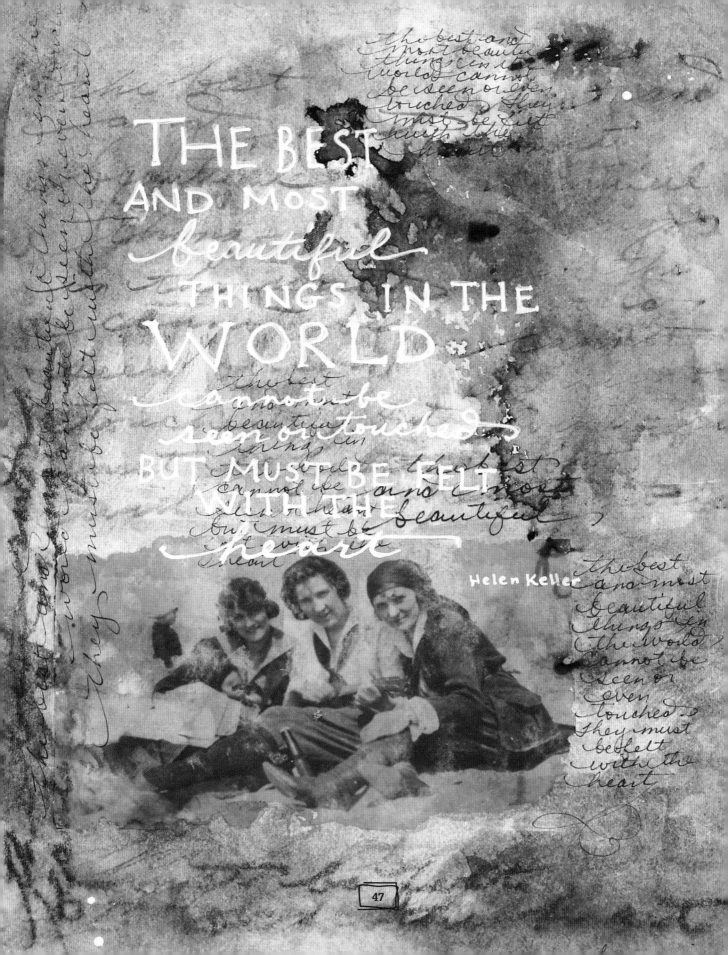

THE BEST AND MOST *beautiful* THINGS IN THE WORLD cannot be seen or touched BUT MUST BE FELT WITH THE *heart*

Helen Keller

PENS

We all have our favorites. Black fine-line pens, such as the ones made by Micron (in a 0.5 size or smaller) are mine. They're great for adding dense, detailed sections of writing, and the 0.5 size seems to hold up well. I'm also fond of some of the paint markers on the market. They flow over layers like a dream.

WALNUT INK

My favorite art supply, these crystals mix with water to create a lovely brown ink. It is water soluble and lends itself well to many layering techniques.

CONTE CRAYONS

A mixture of graphite and clay, these square sticks are classic tools for sketching and drawing and they are perfect for layering. They're made with rich, vibrant pigments in a wide variety of colors. My favorites are the natural tones of sepia, sanguine, sienna and natural umber, but I'm fast becoming a fan of the brighter colors as well.

CHARCOAL

Charcoal comes both compressed in sticks and in pencil form. It makes a lovely texture and adds a lot of depth, especially when paired with other media.

WATER-SOLUBLE CRAYONS

This medium can be used in a myriad of ways, from loose lettering to rich applications of color. Water-soluble crayons are great unifying tools, because just a little water blends them nicely with surrounding elements. They are best applied last, however, because it can be difficult to letter over them.

Now that you've seen how to use many tools to create letterforms, why not try combining some of them together to make one mixed-media piece? Who'd have thought letters could be this much fun!

Figure 1

Figure 2

Figure 3

Figure 4

Figure 5

Figure 6

Figure 7

SEEING WITH YOUR CREATIVE SIDE

BY MATT LYON

Human vision works by turning things into symbolic icons, and often this prevents us from truly seeing something as it is—and that prevents us from drawing as well as we could. Hopefully this awareness will help you better observe what you are seeing when you are drawing, painting, photographing or making whatever sort of visual art you make.

Apparently our brains consist of right and left halves, the left brain being the logical, analytical part and the right brain being the emotional and creative part. When we hear our thoughts as words, we are using our left brains, and most of us spend a lot of time thinking this way. This is good, because otherwise we'd have to resort to grunting or pantomime to communicate with others.

As good as words are, however, they can be problematic for artists. The left brain likes to give names to things, and the instant we assign something a name we no longer see it as it is, but rather as the abstract metaphor, or symbolic icon, of the name we've given it. But it doesn't have to be this way. I'm going to share with you a drawing secret.

Drawing well involves seeing a thing as it is, not as what our left brain tells us it is. You have to look past seeing "a hand" or "a tree" or whatever you are trying to draw and actually look at the thing. Don't come up with adjectives. You don't want to draw "a tall brown tree with bushy green leaves." Go beyond what words can describe. Look at shapes and contour, look at lighting and texture, look at the negative and the positive space, look at everything except the words your left brain is telling you the thing is. Look at it until you become obsessed with such minute details that you can't possibly describe what you see with words. At this point you are seeing things as they are. You are seeing with your right brain.

Not only will seeing with your right brain help you better render things naturalistically, it also will improve any kind of visual artwork you may be working on.

The diagram below shows how my left brain "sees" a photograph like the one above. Without looking at the lighting, the texture, the space and the contour, all I can do to picture this scene is fill in the blanks with what the words provide me with. As the saying goes, "A picture is worth a thousand words."

READING LIST

· · · · · · ·

Ways of Seeing by John Berger

Understanding Comics by Scott McCloud
(this is a very good book about all visual art forms, really)

Seeing Is Forgetting the Name of the Thing One Sees: A Life of Contemporary Artist Robert Irwin by Lawrence Weschler

HAT

PLANT

HOUSE WALL

BOY

CHAPS

HORSE

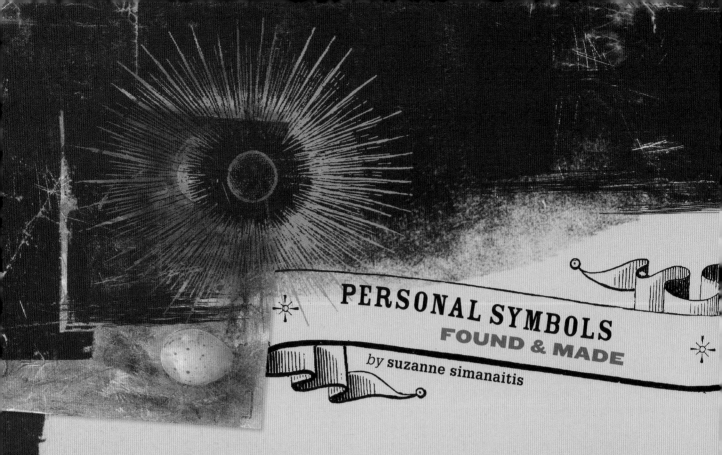

PERSONAL SYMBOLS
FOUND & MADE
by suzanne simanaitis

When I was a little girl—before I got it into my head that I couldn't draw—I loved to draw mailboxes. I have no idea why. But there they are, in all my naively confident, bright scrawls that survive to this day: mailboxes on posts with perky red flags on the side. We didn't even have a mailbox like that, but clearly at some point I must have seen one and it made a huge impression on me, and thereafter every little house with four-square windows and a curly-smoked chimney was accompanied by a mailbox, usually twice the size of anything else in the composition.

I wish I could remember what those mailboxes meant to me. I'd like to say it was something to do with their role as portals for miraculous communication (for at the time I doubt I knew how mail worked and I almost certainly had no awareness of postal carriers), but it was probably something much less profound. I think maybe I just thought the little red flags were cute. I am a sucker for moving parts.

Still, I am curious about this potent symbol so evident in my childhood imagination.

When you put together colors, lines and textures, you are communicating an idea or a point of view to an audience. The message might be as simple as "Hey, these things are cool together," but it's deeply satisfying when the viewer walks away thinking, "Wow, that collage/song/story really resonated with me." If you

want to start a significant dialogue with those who view your creative output (even if it's a conversation you are having exclusively with yourself right now), it helps to include symbols, the pictures that are worth the proverbial thousand words.

We speak and write using words that express certain concepts. We also communicate via images that are symbolic of something else. In the same way that dreaming about broken bones does not mean you should necessarily think twice about riding your bike to the office the next day, the symbols you use in your artwork can be taken literally but are also a shorthand way of expressing a complicated idea or injecting a certain emotion into a composition.

The symbols you use in your artwork lend a richness, a new layer of complexity that may engage different viewers to varying degrees. But it's best not to worry about what people will think or whether they'll "get it." Just as in dream interpretation, there are some symbols that are widely recognized and agreed upon by the collective unconscious, but what matters more than that is what the dreamer thinks the dream means. Your audience might not speak the same symbolic language as you, but if you are fluently speaking your true symbols, it is unlikely that people will look at the work and not be affected by it. They may walk away shaking their heads, thinking "What the heck was that all about?" but at least they are wondering, and your job as the instigator of communication was effective on some level after all.

So, what is your symbolic language, anyway? It's important not to overthink this. You don't have to work on developing your personal mythology because it will emerge when it is ready and you are paying attention. And don't spend a lot of time trying to manipulate or predict how the viewer will react. Spend your attention on your fullest expression of the symbolic content, and let the interpretations come naturally to those who respond to it.

Your personal symbols may already lurk in your artwork. Observe the images that show up frequently. Ask yourself, "Which of these things stand for other things?" What animals are you drawn to? What stories do you want to tell over and over? Your symbols may be there on the canvas right now, but maybe you haven't noticed them or identified what they are there to say. Choose one, and listen to it. Ask yourself what story fragment is being told by that apple or those wings, then see if you can follow a similar thread of meaning through your other artworks and in your dreams.

When you think you know what your symbol is about, try using it intentionally in a series of pieces designed to explore its message. You may find that the symbol says something unexpected.

The more familiar you become with your personal symbols, the more they will grow and change. One day you will put an apple in a collage that you thought would

be far from appleness, yet there it is. Your symbols will take on lives of their own, and they will appear in your work unbidden and in contexts you don't expect, challenging you to examine your assumptions and resume the dialogue. Keep going! This is important. As you grow simply by being engaged in your world, your creative output evolves, and the go-to bits and pieces you've relied on will change, too. You'll add new symbols to your repertoire, and the old ones will fall in and out of favor as you explore different subjects and seek to communicate new messages.

Your personal symbols don't have to be strange or unique objects. In fact, they may be more effective if they are everyday things. Allow yourself to portray cats, to choose houses. What is important is not the image or the object. It is the meaning that you saturate it with. The bones of that cat and the beams of that house are the frameworks over which you can lay different moods and meanings and techniques. As your symbols make return engagements in your artwork you will learn that when the seashell shows up, the story is about home (but some day it may be about brittleness, or about listening).

Symbols are slippery, and you cannot guarantee that your viewers will accurately interpret your meaning—they've got rich imaginary worlds of their own, after all. You might use sewing pattern tissue paper in your collages to symbolize having direction or to pay tribute to women's resourcefulness, but to another person it could carry the baggage of being poor and having to sew your own clothes. Maybe that house in the picture represents the nostalgic safety of childhood. Maybe it stands for financial stability. Maybe it's a dollhouse, too perfect and artificial to be trusted, or merely a façade that will tumble in the slightest breeze—nothing safe about that.

A lot of us use birds as symbols in our artwork. Hey, they're easy to draw! To me, birds always look inquisitive and a little nervous. I suppose birds represent courage or a freedom from earthbound reality, yet we frequently depict them just standing around. So is it communicating something other than its obvious loitering birdness or not? Whatever shorthand you intend your symbols to communicate, be sure of it in your own mind and represent it accordingly in your work. It will help your audience "get it" to see that bird soaring if it is meant to imply freedom. Otherwise it might just be in the picture to lend the context of being outside, or to provide a size reference.

That's why I haven't resumed my mailbox kick: I'm not sure what it symbolizes, and I don't want to force it. But when I'm ready to understand it, it will resurface in my artwork. And I will flip the perky little red flag to the "Messages inside!" position.

Sanctuary

FILL A SPACE IN A BEAUTIFUL WAY. ~GEORGIA O'KEEFFE

When you're really feeling it, it's pretty much impossible to keep creative expression confined to a canvas or a studio. It manifests all around you, in the clothes you wear and the meals you cook and the home you keep. Aside from the likelihood that you've got a desk, closet or bedroom that strains to contain a happily chaotic jumble of art supplies, I'd wager that your creativity has expressed itself in terms of interesting juxtapositions of colorful bed linens, ever-changing displays of framed photos along the staircase and weird thingamajigs tucked into bookcases, if not actual artworks on every available surface. I know. We can't help it. It's how we operate.

There are countless incremental ways to turn your home into your sanctuary, to surround yourself with the colors, imagery and objects that make your heart sing and provide an environment that encourages your best work. You may have to compromise with landlords or family members, but even small steps are better than nothing. Something as simple as fresh flowers can add a splash of inspiring color and rhythm (they are wonderful to draw, too).

Ignore trends and let there be one rule to guide your decorating: use what you love. I saw a shower curtain printed with frolicking costumed monkeys, and I loved it so much that I bought two and hung them as regular curtains in my living room. Those little guys, being the mischievous imps you would expect them to be, have taken over the entire room, manifesting as pillows, toys, paintings, lamps and candlesticks. I never would have set out to decorate my sanctuary in a Mid-Century-Monkeys-Wearing-Clothing motif, but there it is, and I adore it, and I bet there is not another room like it anywhere. I let one odd choice lead to another, and eventually it turned out to be a coherent "look" that sneaks up on visitors rather than assaulting them, as I initially feared it might. (Well, I do keep the chair upholstered in Chinese dragon fabric as far across the room as possible from the monkey curtains, because who needs that drama?)

Think of decorating your home with other people's artwork as a karmic investment. You may feel a pinch when you write the check, but you will be grateful for your abundant good fortune every time you look at an artwork you love, and you'll have helped another artist acquire more art supplies—not to mention self-esteem and rent money. It'll come back to you someday. Have your acquisitions professionally framed if they aren't already, and while you're at it, bestow that honor upon a few of your own pieces too. It's uplifting to the creative spirit!

Display artwork and other compelling things in every room so that wherever you come to rest, there is something to engage your creative brain. Tuck a small piece into the linen closet where it can surprise you with its loveliness. Prop a work-in-progress atop the fridge where its unexpected context might help unlock its secrets or reveal areas that need more work.

Even if you prefer a pristine studio of unadorned white walls, gather and display precious objects somewhere nearby, where your hungering eyes and imagination may feast as necessary. By collecting and displaying objects that you love, you come face to face with your own personal aesthetic and your unique symbolic language emerges. The dapper little monkeys have not infiltrated my artwork yet, but I expect it any day now.

artwork at left:
PAM COFFMAN, TRACI BUNKERS, MATT AND KATE LYON, RANDI FEUERHELM-WATTS

Purging for Peace

by MARILEE FOSBRE

In a job I once held, we sometimes had clients with such severe hoarding disorders that their homes became unsafe, not to mention totally scary. When this happened we either had to pay someone to clean it out and haul it away or do it ourselves. We called this odious job a "dig-out."

Years later, there came a day when I came home from teaching a couple of mixed-media classes, dumped all my crates of supplies on the studio counters and left them there. I couldn't face putting them away because the whole studio was packed with junk and clutter and any hope of organization was long gone.

Around this time I also learned that I had been accepted to graduate school and would need a fresh space for studying in the fall. I looked around, aghast, and sighed, "Dig-out!" As incentive I decided to have a sale at the end and, with the profits, reward myself by buying a really cool soldering iron.

I worked backward, visualizing what I wanted my life and space to be like when I was finished—a soothing absence of clutter and a calm space conducive to study and artwork. I imagined keeping only the supplies that I love. Everything else would be purged.

The next step was harder and required a great deal of honest soul-searching. I made lists under such headings as: things I love to do, things I haven't touched in ages, things I thought I would like to do but don't, and things I am simply never going to do.

I admitted to myself that I really don't like altering books, that journaling just isn't for me, that I hadn't made a greeting card or used a rubber stamp in months and that I really hate teaching polymer clay classes. No matter how much I wanted to, I acknowledged that I was never going to

alter that bag of Barbie dolls I bought at a garage sale four years ago. All the supplies and materials for these activities ended up being purged. I also had a list of what I love: SoulCollage (and all other kinds of collage), all my paints, crayons and mediums, vintage ephemera, beads and boxes upon boxes of images. These were my riches and I would keep them.

My old boss used to say when you have to swallow more than one frog, you might as well start with the biggest one, so I started with the dreaded walk-in closet. I chucked every single item into one of three bins: Sale, Keep and Trash. Each time a bin was full I packed the items into boxes for the sale, took the trash to the garage or set aside items to keep. If I was in doubt I referred to my lists, and that helped me be strong as I tucked a pasta machine, a toaster oven and tons of art clay into Sale boxes.

Over the next two months I methodically worked my way around the studio and through the attic using the same sorting process, ever conscious of my determination to keep only what I love to use.

After fifty-one days of weekend and evening work, I completed the dig-out. During this time I excavated the very first greeting card I ever made and rediscovered treasures that I had not laid hands on in years. I had lots of time as I sorted to think about what is important to possess and what is ridiculous, and vowed to remember the difference. I filled the back of a pickup truck with items for the sale and made almost seven hundred dollars sending them on to good homes. I ended up with a serene space that brings joy to my heart when the morning light bounces off the clean counters, where I use my new soldering iron without hindrance.

Priority: URGENT. Cleared for IMMEDIATE RELEASE! An insidious new disease, Obsessive Compulsive Designer Syndrome, has just been identified. Although OCDS most often infects the female population, research indicates that it occurs in both sexes and all age groups.

OCDS manifests itself in the form of addictive behaviors— a constant, obsessive need to redecorate, renovate and remodel both interior and exterior spaces. While often costly and difficult to treat, the disease is easily diagnosed and seldom fatal.

In order to encourage early detection and stop the spread of OCDS, a simple, painless test has been developed that can be administered in the comfort and privacy of your own home. Even if you have no apparent symptoms, you are urged to take the following test to determine if you are at risk for contracting Obsessive Compulsive Designer Syndrome.

AN *INSIDIOUS* NEW DISEASE

by *PAM COFFMAN*

OCDS DIAGNOSTIC TEST

Simply answer YES or NO to the following questions and then check your score to determine if you have OCDS.

1. Have the walls in your house been painted every color of the rainbow at one time or another (or even all at once)?

2. If you see a broken piece of furniture at the curb, do you make an immediate U-turn and pick it up?

3. Does your family have bruised shins or broken toes because you moved the furniture in the middle of the night?

4. Are you a closet decorator (i.e., you have decorated every room in your house and the closets are the only things left to decorate)?

5. Have your children and/or spouse come home and thought they were in the wrong house because everything was different than it was when they'd left that morning?

6. Are you addicted to HGTV, DIY, and HOME programs?

7. Do you buy or subscribe to more than five interior design magazines per month?

8. Do you consider Trash-To-Treasure one word?

9. Do your Internet bookmarks include a whole folder for decorating and gardening?

10. Does your blog mention multiple decorating tips?

11. Does your Amazon "wish list" automatically update itself when a new decorating book comes out?

12. When you take decorating quizzes and you're asked to select your favorite style do you usually choose, (C) All of the above?

DETERMINING YOUR TEST RESULTS

Yes to 2-3 questions: You are very likely to become infected with OCDS.

Yes to 4-5 questions: You are already in the preliminary stages of OCDS.

Yes to 6-8 questions: You should begin treatment immediately.

Yes to 9 or more questions: It's too late for you, because you are probably rearranging the furniture, painting the room or making new curtains instead of determining your score on this test anyway.

OCDS is not covered by HMOs, Medicare or other health insurance plans. Consequently, limited budgets and a lack of understanding on the part of spouses, families and friends force many OCDS sufferers into a state of withdrawal, and believe me, it is not pretty!

However, there is good news concerning treatment for people inflicted with OCDS. Although there are no treatments acknowledged by the AMA and no medications approved by the FDA, I have successfully treated my own case of OCDS with Collage Therapy or CT. Because OCDS is associated with addiction and compulsion, this is not a cure—relapse can occur—but this course of treatment has proven 95 percent effective. The cost is minimal and the procedure is painless and even enjoyable. The goal of CT is to redirect the obsessive urges into a similar though less invasive activity.

OVERVIEW OF THE CT TREATMENT REGIME

The first step is the most difficult: take a pair of scissors and cut up your interior design, redecorating and gardening magazines. I know this is overwhelming, but trust me, you can do this. Be advised, this is not random destructive cutting it is purposeful, creative cutting. Find images of rooms that you would love to live in (the charming English cottage, the elegant manicured country estate or the sleek modern steel-and-glass entryway of your dreams) and accessories that you have been dying to buy (chairs, tables, sofas, beds …). Later, as you become more confident, try cutting up your *Oprahs*, *Marthas*, *Verandas* and *Elle Decors*. (Caution: Do this gradually, or the shock may be too much.)

Next, set up a system to categorize and store the images. My categories are furniture, accessories and textures; interior rooms; building exteriors/façades; doors, windows and stairs;

gardens/nature; people and pets. The images are stored in large plastic bins in my studio. At this point, I must confess that cutting and sorting the images can itself become addictive, but it is less expensive and exhausting than OCDS—*and* you can do it while watching HGTV.

When the irresistible urge to paint or wallpaper strikes, simply go to your stash and pull out several images from each category. This can be a random process or you can select images by theme or color. Look through the images and select pieces that inspire you at that moment. Then begin creating the "room" of your dreams, adding furnishings, selecting the exteriors and designing wonderfully effortless gardens out of the bits and pieces of the images. You are the builder, designer, decorator and landscaper with total artistic control of what will go into your creation. If you have an image with a color that doesn't work, find a marker and change it. If you want to use stuff from all of the categories, go right ahead—it is *your* design.

Now rather than reaching the limit on your credit cards and risking overexertion from the rigors of renovation, refocus this creative compulsion into making a collage. After you have a design direction, cut a piece of illustration board or get a stretched canvas and begin the process of arranging the images into a unified composition. Once you are satisfied with the design, use a suitable glue to secure the pieces to the support. Consider including bits of decorative papers or even some of those wallpaper samples you hoarded for just the right project. Paint, markers, colored pencils, oil pastels and chalk can be used to enhance or change colors and help create a flow from one image to the next. The collage can be highly impressionistic or as realistic as you wish.

The exterior, interior and garden of your dreams *can* coexist in the same space—first, in your imagination, and now in your collage. Imagine who would live in this space you've created. Or choose someone, maybe a favorite literary character, artist or celebrity and create the type of space you would envision them in. Remember, there are no rules—this is therapy.

Apart from significant and lasting reduction in OCDS patients' addictive behavior, Collage Therapy provides economic benefits to them and their families. Compared to traditional treatments such as psychotherapy, medication and chiropractic care for all those muscles pulled while moving furniture and climbing ladders, CT contributes to significant cost savings. For sufferers who have not been diagnosed, who refuse treatment or are in a state of denial, the cost of feeding their addiction can be staggering. Collage Therapy can significantly reduce these costs. For example, the price of one chair for the family room can average seven hundred dollars, one hundred times more than the cost of just one decorating magazine that will supply *numerous images* of chairs. Research has shown that CT is effective in reducing the symptoms of OCDS, improving relationships and self-esteem. Please, get out those scissors and magazines and take your first step on the journey to recovery today.

a dream *creative space*

BY MARNEY K. MAKRIDAKIS

As with the creation of any piece of art, creating a dream creative space begins with having a vision. Of course, there will be wonderful twists and turns of spontaneous serendipity along the way. But knowing what you want is the powerful key to having it.

DEVELOP THE VISION OF YOUR STUDIO

Use your favorite media and techniques to create a representation of your ideal space for creative working and playing. Refer to the previous article by Pam Coffman for great instructions on how to create a collage depicting this ideal space.

I created a collage of my ideal writing office. I wanted it to be orange and yellow, cozy and happy, and a cross between a playroom, an art studio and a chic cottage. The space that I manifested is startlingly similar to what I envisioned in my collage! Take a look at these pictures. The "before" is the collage of my ideal writing office, and the "after" is a photo of my manifested creative space!

That dream space of yours.

Make it real.

EXAMINE YOUR BELIEFS RELATED TO MANIFESTING THE STUDIO
A day or two later, return to your collage.

1. In stream-of-consciousness style, write a full page of thoughts, about why you don't think you can have the beautiful space you visualized in your collage. Write quickly and don't worry about it being messy. Write about what seems unrealistic and selfish, and why you believe those things. Fill up the whole page.

2. Now, turn this piece of paper 180 degrees so that the writing just looks like a bunch of unintelligible scrawls. Allow your right brain to scan the page and see symbols, patterns, new words and other secret messages, hiding amid the scribbles. If you don't see anything at first, squint your eyes and look some more. Think abstractly, not literally.

3. Allow what you see on the rotated page to inspire you to write, draw, doodle, sketch, paint or alter the page in any way, to depict why manifesting your dream studio is possible. There's no "right" way to do this. Be spontaneous!

To hold this kind of emotion related to something you want, you must be very clear about *why* you want it. Once that sense is very much alive, you'll be able to figure out ways to integrate that essence into your daily life.

PINPOINT AND INTEGRATE THOSE ESSENCES

1. Do a quick "lightning-round" on **why** you want that "dream studio" you've envisioned. Think about how you will **feel** when you achieve it.

2. Next, write a short paragraph in which you are the main character. Write about being in your dream creative space in a very specific way, emphasizing the details in the room and how they make you feel.

Here is an example:
Marney walks into the room and instantly feels uplifted because of the sky-blue walls that mirror the sky that's visible through the picture window that takes up the entire front wall. She allows her fingers to run through the soft bristles of the premium sable paintbrushes that are meticulously hung on the enchanting antique spice rack, which makes her feel proud and sophisticated. She smiles when she sees the drafting table in pristine condition, and feels like she is finally a "real artist." The classical music on the state-of-the-art sound system fills her with a sense of true freedom and bliss.

3. When you are finished writing a detailed story, go back and rewrite it, keeping everything as-is, but replacing the dream room details with things that are already within your reach right now.

4. On a big piece of posterboard, make a "blueprint" (or a purple-print, a fuchsia-print, or a lilac-print) of what you'll do to integrate these ideas into your life **now**. Create two columns: one for "essences" (basic truths about your creative space that you've discovered are important to you) and another for "things" (the tangibles that you've dreamed of to furnish and manifest your creative space) and under each column, create a space for "actions" (specific steps you can take to integrate those things in your life sooner rather than later). Using the previous example, I could have discovered the following:

Essences
Feeling uplifted, pride, sophistication, feeling like a "real" artist, freedom and bliss

Essence-Actions
Take more pride in my work, treat my art time more seriously, call myself an "artist" more often, give myself permission for more freedom in my life

Things
Sky-blue walls, picture window, high-quality brushes, antique brush rack, pristine drafting table, classical music, state-of-the-art sound system

Thing-Actions
Paint one wall blue, add curtains to the window, save up loose change to invest in quality brushes, browse eBay for a spice rack, play classical music while I'm creating art

Once these plans are written down, have fun with this "blueprint" poster. Express yourself with paints and collage materials. Create it in a way that you will love to look at it and have it as a constant, compassionate reminder of the changes that are to come. Allow the very act of making this poster to fill your creative well with the light of possibility!

You will now have a vision of what you want in a creative space, a reframing of the beliefs that have been standing in your way and a checklist for integrating the aspects of your dream space that you can have *now*. Your creative space is an aspect of your creative personality. The space of your dreams *can* be yours!

ART DANS LA BOUDOIR

by Traci Bunkers

I normally make art standing at my art table, listening to loud music and dancing. That is, unless it's wintertime. In winter, I find myself mysteriously drawn to my bed—a temptress beckoning to me to crawl under her flannel-covered duvet and never leave. To compromise, I have learned to multitask. I can be comfortable in my flannel nest, watch movies and make art all at the same time.

You have to think "less is more." You can't drag all of your art supplies onto your bed. Well, you could, but don't. Once you get situated with too much stuff, you won't be able to move or get up. I have a small art box that is perfect for making art in bed. It has a small pair of scissors, a few rubber stamps, ink pads, crayons, watercolors, pens, markers, tape, a glue stick and wet wipes. I also keep a few plastic envelopes full of collage and photo fodder. You will also want a few acrylic paints (I said a *few*), a small water container, a paintbrush or two and a couple paper towels.

My favorite art-making-in-bed accessory? An inexpensive breakfast tray with folding legs. It has a small lip around the top so that the art tools won't roll off. The folding legs are nice because you can fold them up and store the whole kit and caboodle under the bed. Then, when the muse visits, you are ready to go. Look for a tray with a lip

around it that isn't too high. If it is, it'll be hard to work on. In bed, I normally work in my visual journal which just about takes up the whole tray. Since there isn't much room left over for supplies, and it's hard to have supplies loose on the bed, I put other items on another small tray.

So far (knock on wood), I've never had a spill or gotten anything on my duvet or bed. But if you are messy or are afraid that might happen, you could put something water-proof on top of your bedspread to protect it. A cheap plastic tablecloth or shower curtain liner would be great. Since I'm an avid recycler, I always have a stack of catalogs and magazines around. When I need to glue something, I put it face down in an opened catalog or magazine and cover the back of it with glue stick or gel medium. When I'm ready to glue something else, I just turn the catalog page. That keeps the glue mess contained and it can still be recycled when it's all glued up.

I can hear it now. Some of you are crying out, "But I've got a partner and I can't take up their side of the bed with art stuff." Don't fret. This gives you all the more reason to remember that you don't need a lot of supplies to have artistic fun. Encourage your partner to make art also and share the supplies. You can put some of the supplies on nightstands.

Now, art-making in bed would not be complete without some good movies. Think colorful and inspirational. Here's a list of movie recommendations (in no particular order) that I think are good for making art. I haven't seen all of these—I asked some friends to contribute their favorite picks as well. Don't forget the popcorn, and keep the remote handy!

MOVIE CHECKLIST

☐ FRIDA—A very beautiful movie about the Mexican painter, Frida Kahlo.

☐ SUPERSTAR: THE LIFE AND TIMES OF ANDY WARHOL—A documentary on Andy Warhol, from childhood to death.

☐ MOULIN ROUGE—A colorful, offbeat musical about the underworld of Paris's Moulin Rouge in 1899.

☐ BASQUIAT—The story of Jean-Michel Basquiat, a street artist discovered by Andy Warhol, and the toll that success took on his life.

☐ VINCENT & THEO—The story of Vincent van Gogh and his relationship with his brother. It also shows the picturesque locations where he painted.

☐ SURVIVING PICASSO—Focusing on François Gilot, a young painter who becomes one of Picasso's women, this tells the story of her life with him and how she "survives" to have a life of her own.

☐ POLLOCK—A portrayal of Jackson Pollock's tormented life, from the time he met his wife, through to his death.

☐ STEALING BEAUTY—In scenic Tuscany, a young poet tries to find answers to some questions about her mother while spending the summer in an artist's refuge.

☐ CAMILLE CLAUDEL—A biography of a young sculptor who becomes the mistress of Auguste Rodin, and her struggle to escape his shadow.

☐ WHAT DREAMS MAY COME—A very colorful movie about wonderful and dark places of the afterlife, featuring Robin Williams.

☐ WAKING LIFE—An interesting movie about a man trying to tell the difference between his waking life and his dreamworld.

☐ CRUMB—A documentary showing a glimpse into the strange mind and life of cartoonist R. Crumb through interviews of those around him and through his comic work.

☐ NEW YORK STORIES—Three different stories by three different directors, with the most fascinating one about a successful artist and his struggles with ego and isolation.

☐ WHITE OLEANDER—About a teenager sent from foster home to foster home and all that she experiences after her mother is sent to prison for a crime of passion. (Watch for the Polaroid transfers and suitcase assemblage.)

☐ CARNIVAL OF SOULS—A very surreal Twilight Zone-esque movie with incredible visuals and spookily whimsical characters. Filmed in the 1960s in my town!

MAGICK *portable shrine*

BY MATT AND KATE LYON

If you want something to decorate your workspace (your desk, your drawing table—anywhere, really) that is fun and easy to make and is perhaps a bit more interesting than your standard picture frame, try this folding paper project.

The Magick Portable Shrine stands about 9" (23cm) tall with a 1" (3cm) deep shelf. The area above the shelf holds a 3" × 5" (8cm × 13cm) photograph or piece of artwork. Photocopy the provided pattern on the opposite page for the basic structure, then add your own ornamental elements to create the façade.

WHAT YOU WILL NEED

- *heavyweight cardstock*
- *scissors and/or a utility knife*
- *tape or glue or something to stick two pieces of the cardstock together*
- *stylus or a bone folder for scoring/ creasing the cardstock (optional)*
- *stuff to decorate your shrine*

1. Photocopy the shrine template onto one sheet of cardstock.
2. Cut out the shrine structure shape. Cut along all of the solid lines, including the middle part for the shelf, the tabs on the shelf, and the slots for the tabs on the side panels.
3. Folding time! Make valley folds on the dashed lines and mountain folds on the dash-dotted lines. You might want to use a stylus or a bone folder to score the lines before folding.
4. Insert the tabs through the slots, fold them if you haven't already, and glue or tape them to their side panels.
5. The shrine should stand up on its own now. If you've used sturdy cardstock, you'll find that the shelf can hold small items, some of which might even be quasi-heavy.

6. Decorate it. If you photocopied the columnar decorations or some other decorative stuff, cut it all out and attach it. Be creative! This is *your* shrine, after all. You might want to try making the interior backdrop removable—then you'll have a multipurpose shrine that you can change as the mood strikes. If you wish, you can make it hangable by punching a hole (and perhaps reinforcing it) in the back of the shrine structure. Nail it to your studio wall, or tack it up in your office cubicle. Wherever you display your shrine, use it to focus your creative intentions on something worthwhile.

✳ P.S. UH, WE DON'T RECOMMEND BURNING A CANDLE ON THIS.

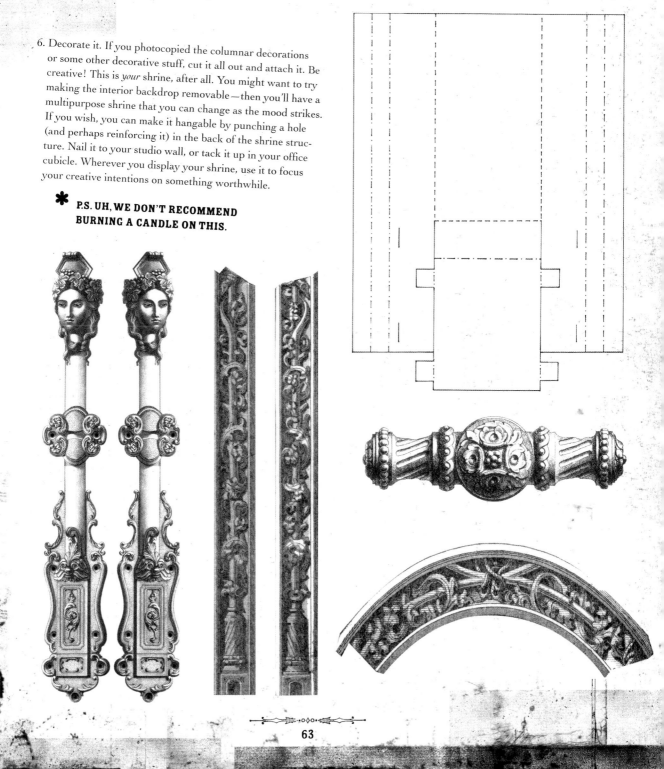

DRESSMAKER

by SONJI HUNT

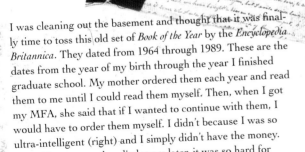

I was cleaning out the basement and thought that it was finally time to toss this old set of *Book of the Year* by the *Encyclopedia Britannica*. They dated from 1964 through 1989. These are the dates from the year of my birth through the year I finished graduate school. My mother ordered them each year and read them to me until I could read them myself. Then, when I got my MFA, she said that if I wanted to continue with them, I would have to order them myself. I didn't because I was so ultra-intelligent (right) and I simply didn't have the money.

When my mother died years later, it was so hard for me to get rid of them, even though they had moved to the basement and weren't regular reading material for me. They survived a couple of spring floods because they were high on shelves and I would page through them every so often. Lots of books, lots of history, so much change in the world.

This summer, I still tried to save them, but they have that lingering damp-basement smell. I gave them one final read, focusing on the *Year in Fashion* sections. The articles were usually short, sometimes only three or four short paragraphs, with a small photo or two. My mother always said, "History repeats itself, even in fashion." And of course, she was right. In the late '70s, early '80s, I loved to wear her 1940s suit jackets. She told me that '40s fashion was reminiscent of some Victorian styling—like the big shoulder pads and peplums and narrow waists. Thank goodness the bustle didn't reinvent itself! Looks from the mid to late '60s and early '70s were taken from flapper fashion. That great '80s stuff drew from some of the '50s looks, and so on. I see trends now of styles that I wore when I was a little girl, except teens and grown women are wearing them—scary! Nothing is really ever a new idea, just bits and pieces recycled. I guess my mother really was always right.

FASHION:

Fashion Passion: Find Your Style

My Mother was such a fashionable individual. Long before designer clothing was available to the general public, she would sew her own outfits from Vogue patterns or even design her own gowns, dresses, suits or casual wear from patterns that she made herself. When I was a little girl she taught me to sew, by hand, create patterns and alter designs to suite my own fashion sense. I practiced with scraps of the beautiful materials that she had collected from all over the world during her youthful travels. My Mother had her own classic, yet crazy style. I think that mine is just crazy. Maybe if I can get focused....

SHAPE
TEXTURE
MOVEMENT
FUNCTION

What is else have I learned from watching a week of makeover TV (aside from I never want a makeover because I hate to wear make up!!)

BOLD PATTERNS seem to always be in style and are used to conceal what are perceived as figure flaws.

SOFT, FLUID LINES always make a woman feel pretty and soft and girly and also hide stuff that you dont particularly care for on your figure like a big rear end or a small rear end or narrow hips or large hips or large thighs or skinny thighs or flat chest or huge chest or no waistline or ....ANYTHIN?!!!

SOFT SKIRTS WITH MOVEMENT...WRAP SKIRTS seem to get chosen for fancy occasions and most women dont like the fact that the skirt flies open...a double wrap or panel wrap skirt is a better choice.

COLOR OF THE SEASON (according to Andre on The TODAY Show)....well, none of the fashionistas on the makeover shows were going for WHITE. They were all about COLOR COLOR COLOR. Maybe a lot of these shows were taped before Andre told us what we should be wearing.

Middles

by Randi Feuerhelm-Watts

An environmental artist by the name of Andy Goldsworthy did an installation artwork piece called *Three Cairns*. Inspired after a trip to Iowa, he was intrigued by the American Midwest and its relationship to the two coasts. Do you know why? It fell in the middle. Drawing an imaginary line through the continent, he built three cairns (large, symbolic stone markers): two in tidal zones just off the coasts of California and New York, and one smack dab in the middle, on the Iowa prairie.

Reading about this project made me think about middles. Half-a-cup. A middle child. Midlife. Halfway through a book. Middle of the road. Being interrupted in the middle of a conversation. Middle school. Middle class …

After moving to Iowa I was talking to my oldest son on the phone one day and he asked, "So where is Iowa, Mom? Somewhere in the middle?" Middles—they all seem so … so-so, don't they? No one ever wants to sit in the middle

seat of a plane or be the middle child. It's like getting a C on a test. I have yet to meet anyone that really wants to play center field. It seems that all the middles have one thing in common. You are neither halfway here nor halfway there.

My new neighbor Andrew has lived here in Iowa all his life and will turn eighteen next month. As a result, he is filled with Midwestern culture wisdom. He says Iowa is "average."

There is something secure about living at the coastal edge of the country. *California*. It's like *Friday*—it's on the end, it's definite. When you

hear the word *Friday* there is a feeling of excitement and anticipation. It's a happy feeling. Now say *Wednesday* out loud. How did that make you feel? See what I mean? It's like living in Iowa—middles. Honestly, you could blend together all the states around me and I wouldn't notice. Nothing blends with California.

Dear Isaac,

In the news today, apparently there was a lady who was so pissed at her new haircut, that she shot her hairdresser. She returned to the salon asking for her one hundred dollars back and the hairdressre gave it to her, but when the hairdresser tried to leave for the day, the bad-hair chick shot at her car. The news showed the police hand-cuffing the bad-hair chick and of course you know what everyone was looking at.

Reasons I have been too depressed to call anyone back:
1. The lady next door asked us to come over at 6:15 for rhubarb pie. *Six fifteen.* Bret assured me, "We don't have to stay, just eat the pie and leave." I asked Bret what the whole fifteen thing was about, and he said everybody eats at 5:00 and they should be done by 6:00 . . . so it makes sense to have dessert at 6:15.
2. Bret made me stand out in the rain tonight with a flashlight to hold the coffee can while he collected worms for his fishing trip. He kept telling me how much money he was saving us. I kept telling him I would give him the two bucks to buy some worms if he would let me go inside.
3. For fun yesterday we drove thirty minutes out of town to the *Super* Wal-Mart.
4. I find myself uttering ten words that I have never said before in my entire life: "It's almost time to pick the tassels off the corn." I have no idea what it means, but everyone is saying it, so I am saying it too.
5. I can divide my life into two parts: *Before* and *After*:

> *Before:* Flip-flops
> *After:* Thermal socks
>
> *Before:* Salad bars with mixed greens, fresh fruit and avocados
> *After:* Salad bars with iceberg lettuce, gelatin desserts and Thousand Island dressing
>
> *Before:* Surf Report
> *After:* Farm Report
>
> *Before:* Hummers and convertible BMWs
> *After:* Buicks and Chevy trucks
>
> *Before:* Driving forty-five minutes to get anywhere
> *After:* Driving forty-five minutes only for vacation
>
> *Before:* High-speed car chases
> *After:* Who won the high school football game
>
> *Before:* Going out to dinner at 10:00 p.m.
> *After:* Going to bed at 8:00 p.m.

Hope your haircuts are turning out OK. I miss you so much.

Love, Mommy

ART, HEALING + AWARENESS

by Wendy Cook

My work is constantly evolving. Exactly what it is evolving into remains unclear. Perhaps it will come full circle. I guess that is part of the mystery of it all. What I do know, however, is there was a definitive point at which it changed direction.

My home/studio is across from the former World Trade Center. On 9/11/01, I experienced horrors unimaginable. The resulting trauma made it difficult for me to paint. When I'm painting, I lose myself completely in my work. After 9/11, this sense of being "lost" in my work made me feel vulnerable. I felt like I needed to be alert and ready to react at all times. I didn't want to go outside and face the sights, the smoke, the smells and the sadness.

Still, I knew I needed to remain creative and I would have to find a new form of expression. I needed to free myself from feeling trapped and anxious. I decided to explore two mediums, Polaroid SX-70 manipulation and Polaroid transfers. These two very different mediums required me to get outside and look for images—to focus on the things I loved about my city rather than the devastation outside my home.

The result was not only a new body of work, but also a more positive outlook.

My uncle gave me his old SX-70 camera and off I went. I wandered the Greenmarket, waiting for the light to fall perfectly on the apple cart. The quaint little bakery that felt more like a grandmother's kitchen than a storefront became the subject of one shoot. The smell of vanilla and the surreal pastel icings were a feast for my senses. I indulged in a chocolate cupcake with lavender icing as a reward for my efforts. July brought sunflowers into the lobby of my building, which resulted in a tiny van Gogh. You can imagine my surprise when, on another shoot, my toy truck in the courtyard transformed itself into a real truck on a country lane.

On a morning walk, I photographed a quirky old diner. We called it the "Unch" because of the missing "L" on the sign. This photo is very special to me as the building collapsed shortly after I shot it, due to a possible stress fracture from 9/11. One evening my husband, Robert, and I discovered an old glider bolted to the sidewalk in Tribeca. We sat and rocked. I returned the following day and photographed that too. I realized I was documenting things that brought me joy, a visual reminder of what I loved about my city.

I captured images and then sat patiently on the sidewalk, smearing the emulsion. The film for the SX-70 camera (Polaroid Time-Zero film) has a flaw. It takes a bit of time for the emulsion to harden, which means it can smear and "ruin" an otherwise "perfect" photo. The funny thing about art is that one person's problem can become another's muse. As such, artists all over the world are having a ball experimenting with this film, warming the prints against their bodies and using impromptu tools to swirl and scratch the emulsion between the film's layers.

I enjoyed the immediacy, and also the mystery. I never knew exactly what I would get, but in the end I was left sitting on the sidewalk with a palm-sized impressionistic jewel. I love the painterly look of these tiny photographs, so I began printing them on large canvases.

I was having so much fun with this medium that I then decided to experiment with Polaroid transfers. Armed with an old Polaroid 180 that I found on eBay, a towel, watercolor paper and a thermos of hot water, I set out to photograph a particular corner on Fifth Avenue, making the transfers right there on the sidewalk. I photographed my subject and gave it some time to develop. I peeled apart the film, discarded the back and placed the peel on top of a piece of watercolor paper that I had saturated with hot water from my thermos. After some rubbing, I was able to remove the peel and see the results. More surprises!

One Sunday I spotted a wooden bench under a dogwood tree in full bloom. I returned on my bike, my gear secured to the back in an old picnic basket. My little bike trip yielded a postcard-sized rendering of Wagner Park. Unlike the SX-70 manipulations, this medium results in instant miniature watercolor paintings.

I choose subjects that I find charming or that bring me joy. I create images that evoke a sense of curiosity or nostalgia in the viewer. The angles, lighting and cropping are an integral part of each composition. I am constantly in awe of the creative process, its healing qualities and the fact that its very nature is so difficult to define. To describe my own creative process I would have to say it's part imagination and part intuition, but mostly being aware. I think Henry Miller said it best: "The aim of life is to live, and to live means to be aware, joyously, drunkenly, serenely, divinely aware."

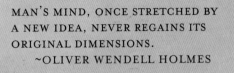

Imagination

Years ago in her excellent zine *Pisces Rising*, Terry Lee Getz introduced me to the concept of the Idea Farm. In TL's parlance, it means a state of mind where simple ideas are allowed to flourish extravagantly, given a little sunshine, irrigation and enough space and time to learn to leap, tumble and multiply. I had always thought of this as an accidental flight of fancy, but I appreciate TL's suggestion that this condition could be a reliable, repeatable process for idea generation to nourish both written and visual creative work.

Idea farming is sort of like when you're with your best friend and you complain about something stupid, and your best friend laughs at you extrapolates your minor concern into something comical, it snaps you out of your funk and, before long, both of you are building on the story in breathless gasps as you brainstorm, improvise and giggle yourselves half to death. It becomes exponentially funnier as it grows more serious and convoluted, and your imaginations are free connect all the crazy scenarios that come barreling forth as you hop onto trains of thought you'd ordinarily never ride. Honestly, if this never happens to you, you need some new friends, because this is just about the most fun two people can have in a vertical position.

The best thing about idea farming is that you can do it all by yourself. Put those crazy voices inside your head to good use, for once, and practice turning mundane observations into full-blown riots of pure imagination. Let one weird-looking mannequin lead you to discover the secret pageantry of the shopping mall after all the humans have locked up and gone home (oh, the dancing!). Or as you toss that apple core into the trash, be the worm and join it on its adventure all the way to the landfill and beyond (make sure to get swept up in a cyclone at some point—why not?).

These mental exercises have obvious benefits for writers; they are extremely valuable for visual artists too. Once you have witnessed the worm's-eye view, your collages may take on a whole new perspective as your color palette slowly tilts. Having cavorted through the mall at midnight with a luxuriously mustachioed mannequin, you will never again plop a doll into a static assemblage. Your imagination simply won't allow it.

Ideas propagated in this manner don't have to be fully mature before you can harvest them to start your artwork. They will ripen and sometimes even cross-pollinate while you play. This, alone, is a worthwhile realization: although there is satisfaction in feeling confident about your ability to manifest your creative vision, it can be thrilling to begin work without any notion of how it will end because your train of thought hasn't reached the terminal yet. And as you have probably noticed, in my hands Terry Lee's farming allegory has become genetically modified into a transportation metaphor—a whole different superfood for your brain to chew on. That's exactly how one idea leads to another.

VEIL

word through art

K. MAKRIDAKIS *artwork by* DEB SILVA

It's healthy for people who express their creativity visually to stretch their writing "legs" occasionally and, likewise, for writers to confront visual material every now and then. The following exercises provide a way for you to dive into exploration of the written word through visual art.

Use the writing prompts that have been paired with the following collages, or try using similar prompts with your own artwork. Combining words and art can be exciting. You may even decide to submit your combination of words and art for publication in an art zine. Happy writing!

WHAT IS THIS WOMAN TRYING TO TELL YOU?

WHERE HAS THIS WOMAN TRAVELED?

WHAT IS HER BIGGEST SECRET?

WHAT PART OF YOU DOES SHE KNOW ABOUT THAT NOBODY ELSE DOES?

WHAT DID SHE DREAM LAST NIGHT?

WHAT WAS THE LAST THING THAT MADE HER CRY?

WHAT LETTER IS SHE PUTTING OFF WRITING?

WHAT COLOR ARE HER SIGHS?

WHAT HAS THIS WOMAN FORGOTTEN?

WHAT CRIME IS SHE GUILTY OF?

IN WHAT WAYS ARE YOU AND SHE SOUL SISTERS?

WHAT WISH WILL SHE MAKE ON THE STARS TONIGHT?

WRITE DOWN THE RECIPE OF INGREDIENTS NEEDED TO COOK HER LAUGH.

IF YOU WERE SITTING TOGETHER SOMEWHERE, WHERE WOULD YOU BE?

WHILE SITTING THERE, WHAT WOULD SHE WHISPER?

WHO ARE THESE WOMEN?

WHICH WOMAN IS WISER, AND WHY?

WHO WAS IN LOVE WITH BOTH WOMEN?

WHO ELSE IS INVITED TO A PARTY GIVEN BY THE THREE OF YOU?

WHAT ARE YOU CELEBRATING?

IF THESE TWO WOMEN SPOKE TO ONE ANOTHER IN A MADE-UP LANGUAGE, WHAT WOULD IT SOUND LIKE?

WHAT WOULD BE THE TRANSLATION OF THE CONVERSATION?

WHAT IS THE BEST GIFT YOU COULD OFFER EITHER OR BOTH WOMEN?

IF SHE COULD HAVE DINNER WITH ANYONE, WHO WOULD SHE CHOOSE?

WHAT IS HER BIGGEST REGRET?

WHAT WOULD IT FEEL LIKE TO SPEND A DAY IN HER BODY?

HOW WOULD IT FEEL FOR HER TO SPEND A DAY IN YOUR BODY?

WHAT ODD HABITS DOES SHE HAVE WHILE SLEEPING?

HOW CAN YOU TELL WHEN SHE IS LYING?

WHAT IS HER GREATEST TALENT?

WHO HURT HER, JUST YESTERDAY?

WHAT HAS THIS GIRL SAID TO YOU IN YOUR DREAMS?

WHAT ARE HER WINGS MADE OF?

WHAT IS THE FIRST THING SHE DOES EVERY MORNING?

WHAT DOES HER BEDROOM FLOOR FEEL LIKE?

WHAT IS THE ONE THING SHE COULD NEVER DO WITHOUT?

WHAT DO YOU HAVE THAT SHE DOES NOT HAVE?

WHAT MAKES HER GIGGLE UNCONTROLLABLY?

WHAT MAKES HER BECOME VERY, VERY QUIET?

WHO ARE HER FAMILY MEMBERS?

WHO WOULD SHE SAY IS HER *true* FAMILY?

WHAT MAKES HER FEEL A LITTLE FEARFUL, AND WHY?

WHAT WISDOM COULD YOU OFFER HER?

WHAT IS THE ONE MEMORY SHE WISHES SHE COULD RE-LIVE?

WHAT HAPPENS TO THE EARTH WHEN SHE DANCES?

IF YOU AND SHE WERE TO MERGE INTO ONE PERSON, WHAT WOULD HAPPEN?

IF HER ESSENCE COULD DRIP OUT OF HER FINGERS, WHAT WOULD IT LOOK LIKE?

Stream-Writing

EXPLORING PERSONAL DEPTHS THROUGH STREAM-OF-CONSCIOUSNESS WRITING PRACTICE

BY TERRY LEE GETZ

I slipped into the stream-of-consciousness practice quite unintentionally. After a late night on the phone with my best friend, discussing life, nature, spirituality and the pursuit of happiness, I didn't get enough sleep and was tired the next afternoon. I was in a strange mood and felt as though I were still inside that conversation. An urge to journal emerged, so I curled up on the chaise and got comfy. I allowed myself to move into the feelings I experienced during our talk. With closed eyes, my mind drifted into a daydream and I wrote these words: "I am writing from the space left, the place left by the dream . . ." Words flowed onto the page indiscriminately; at times I wondered what was happening but ended left-brain activity quickly. I relived the content of the previous evening and no matter what feelings, images or words appeared, I allowed them. The process unfolded until the last words were written, whereupon I closed my journal and took a nap.

Generally, my process entails writing when the urge appears, stopping when the work is finished and ignoring the writing for a period of time following completion. This process was particularly necessary with my stream-of-consciousness writing because the content had a depth of intimacy that challenged me and required taking space from it to get perspective. A month passed before I remembered the work and opened my journal to decipher my illegible handwriting.

In transcription, I was surprised by how much I'd written and how the words were more connected to each other than was apparent during my stream-writing session. My words were descriptive, and some words rhymed. What I'd considered random, disparate thoughts, feelings, images and words actually formed a somewhat cohesive account of the conversation. The narrative piqued my curiosity; had I not been there to know better, I'd swear I hadn't authored the piece. The work felt so foreign to anything I'd written before, even my poetry. This writing conveyed not only personal intimacy but also a universal "beyond me" element heretofore unplumbed. I thought the writing was amazing and beautiful, alien and yet somehow familiar. Would others find it so?

I read the prose poem to my soul sister Donna. She cried when she heard it and said, "I always knew you owned these creative depths, but I've never seen you express them before. This is a love letter to yourself, and you've opened the door now and can go back anytime you want to." I embraced her feedback. My next step was to illustrate the writing. I created an eight-page booklet, *Emergere*, and set the project aside.

Months later at the vernal equinox I felt the compulsion to write, grabbed my journal (mid-conversation with my husband!) and stream-wrote about birds, parenthood and childhood. The work is titled *Circling*. I understood the content of this piece, but its spontaneous arrival was a bit of a shock! In the weeks preceding the prose poem eruption, I'd grieved my dad's suicide, enjoyed migrating birds in our backyard and contemplated childhood memories. Where *Emergere* has a cerebral quality, a mixture of sound and thought, Circling feels visceral and active; the two works have nothing in common other than their stream-of-consciousness pattern.

Another stream-writing occurred two months later. I was in a parking lot when I felt that "tickle" warning— something is being born! I'm never without notebook

Finding 151

and pen, so I scribbled furiously in that parking lot, the resultant mystery writing being a re-experiencing of a back-roads adventure to a waterfall in Virginia. I illustrated the prose poem with my own altered photos and published a booklet titled *Finding 151* that I gave to Donna for her birthday.

My purpose in sharing these experiences is to illustrate how spontaneously stream-of-consciousness writing can arise from your subconscious depths, and how you can seduce it intentionally by creating relaxing environments and allowing your mind to gently roam.

If you're already experiencing spontaneous process in your preferred media, it is possible for you to access even deeper levels by practicing stream-writing. For those who feel their interior depths are not getting expression, here are some pathways to consider:

- View your life as a holistic experience. Western civilization loves to compartmentalize, and we are encouraged to keep parts of our being as separate selves. Let yourself explore how your creative side can be brought into more areas of your life than it is in now. If further integration of creativity eludes you, contemplate your Separate Selves and look for the commonality or intention each has at its core.

- Combine personal evolution with your creative expression. This process is easier for some artists than for others. I've taken the hardest, most painful ways to get to where I am now. It does not need to be this way. Envision what you would do creatively if your sole purpose were simply to show your Soul Fullness. Isn't personal evolution, becoming acquainted with our unique gifts and sharing them, what creative expression is about? What are we saving our lives for, anyway? Today is yours and your life is your business and it deserves your full attention, no matter what circumstances or obligations are at work in your present.

- Make some time each day for the most important person in your life—you! This is where stream-writing practice can be helpful. Isn't it pleasant to daydream? Relax into a daydream with your journal on your lap and a writing instrument in your hand.

emergere

whole water wears down water whittles away water erodes the erosion of spirit sunsets pelicans diving splashing finding flashing glimmer fishes tiny fishes long beaked birds on the shoreline making rhythmic patterned footprints water moves forward erasing evidence of humans and nature, sucking out what was previously forced onto land, the perpetual movement of waves, revealing, removing evidence existence permanence alludes us evidence of a previous life, worn smooth by persistent ruthless water and agitation . . . There, I slipped into your daydream for a few minutes and created my own. It was peaceful to relive collecting shells last Sunday to be offered in celebration of the first candle of the Advent wreath. Can you see where several universal themes come into being, in what was an invocation of a December sunset-watching ritual?

- What can be done creatively with stream-writing? Themes that emerge for exploration can be taken into any literary form, including poetry, essay, nonfiction creative writing or journal prompts. Visually, the patterns revealed (bird footprints, tangled seaweed, ruffled shell fragments) can be used and expressed as hand-carved stamps, woven or beaded wearable art pieces, rubbings, line drawings, landscape paintings or impressionist-style pastel work. A photographer might consider a series of shots celebrating water's nature, the evidence of water shown on objects it has affected in various ways, the different, myriad colors of the sea and sky. A parent or teacher could develop a field trip to the beach, discover its wonders and tell stories about different aspects of the ocean and its inhabitants.

- One fantastic benefit of stream-writing is discovering your own personal symbology. Do you find birds recurring in day and night dreams? Water? What about wind, or fire? Earth, crystals, snowflakes? Do you dream of houses, windows, doorways? Archways, tendrils, tight buds, full blooms? Do ladders, shadows and oil slicks in rain puddles fascinate you? What reaches into your head and heart and drags you forward? Wrinkled foreheads, the hollow in your

Close your eyes or look out a nearby window while softening your eyes. Allow your scalp and forehead to relax; allow your jaw to loosen and your shoulders to slacken. Don't grasp your pen in a death grip; rather, cradle it in your hand as you might a newborn's foot or a wine glass. After you've attended to relaxing your body and are comfortable, monitor your thoughts gently. No, not grocery list; no, not homework or due library books. No, not aches and pains; no, not your friend's drama. What about the beach? Ah yes, the sun . . . the sound of swelling waves breaking . . . that twirl of water in a tiny tide pool, twinkling shells, long bird beaks, tiny bird footprints . . . tangled seaweed black bone fragments acrid smell of rotting vegetation, shell pieces ruffled like bird wings delicate spirals erosion parts of a

I am writing from the space left
the place left
by the dream.
The suspension and immersion
of spirit
of pleasure

of unfulfilled desires
the soft edge of confidence
and the chimera of grace
allowing the flow of words
he asked,
"did i turn you onto the
advent wreath?
it is the honoring of stones and
bones and rocks and shells and
crystals on earth"
beyond our understanding...

it's about the atoms and particles
here and there
in and out
up and down
and the surreal beauty of
what comes next

the welcoming of all things

the animals singing
the elements ringing
the rocks celebrating
the humans dancing together
and singing in a circle with one big voice

his voice
leading the call to pagan mystery and
seasonal surrender to the
still days and long dark nights
the ebbs and flows
the tides
the glowing fish
the phosphorous protoplasm

the paired atoms that are
separate yet
one turns when the other turns
light years away

we turn when our souls connect
we lift our eyes to the heavens
we pray to Gabriel and Ariel for
the grace and pleasure of singing crystals
grieving mountains
of wet clam shells and
secret
pear tree
mysteries

child's back? Why? Every object in the universe has meaning attached to it by humankind. Write down what you feel.

- Some readers will find quick entry to the stream of consciousness through music. To see if music works for you, pick a favorite performer or song, relax, listen and see if you are inspired to do stream-writing. Keep trying until you find songs that take you deeper inside—try childhood favorites, classical and movie soundtracks. Perhaps a certain instrument works for you; try harp, flute, cello or perhaps percussion such as rhythmic drumming. Sing or hum nursery rhymes, your grandma's cooking songs or the fireside camp songs from childhood.

It's my belief that stream-writing can be an invaluable aid to personal and spiritual evolution. Practice can expand creativity into the fathoms of subconscious material and facilitate the artist to make deeper, more intimate work. Stream-of-consciousness writing practice can bust creative blocks because its purpose is to allow any expression, no matter what. Practicing can lead to greater self-love and self-esteem, as its focus is accepting "what is" without judgment. Stream-writing can encourage an artist to play and use the imagination that was so natural in childhood. Rekindle the state of awe and wonder that came so easily to you as a child as you daydream and give way to stream-of-consciousness writing practice.

SET YOUR BRAIN ON FIRE

PUTTING CREATIVE IDEAS INTO ACTION

by Jill Jones

Words are fire. They ignite our passions and help us think. Words can lead us to creative ideas and jump start the creative process. Good ideas often ignite from a spark that falls off a mediocre idea. The more ideas we get, the better the chances that some of them will be outstanding, unusual and original. Prime the pump and go for volume. Think often and think a lot! Once we have a surplus of ideas, we can be selective and develop the best.

BrainSpill: A Basic Technique

The brain is a large receptacle filled with a jumble of "stuff." Learn to periodically spill off some of the "stuff" to make room for "new stuff." Then, examine the spillage in a new light and discover new ideas.

Let's say you want to create a new look for your home. Grab a pen and paper. Start spilling off everything that's floating around in your brain related to the word home. Set a timer for ten minutes and spill away.

As an example, here is part of my initial list: homebrewed, happy home, homespun, home wrecker, home theater, home fries, homey, down home, homeowner, homestyle . . .

Ideas fly fast and furious in the beginning. When the pace slows down, take a deep breath and dredge deeper . . . a house is not a home, home sweet home, home for the holidays, on the home front, letters from home, home away from home, hometown girl, home-grown, there's no place like home . . .

At the end of ten minutes the list will be long and your brain will be open to new ideas about home. Circle words or phrases that speak to you. The word "homebrewed" could make you think of beer that is the color of amber, wheat, dark honey or toast. This could inspire a new color scheme ranging from a pale sunny yellow to a deep toasty brown.

The phrase "letters from home" could spark the idea of using text from letters or famous quotes on walls. Or the entire room could be designed around the theme of a favorite quote or favorite writer such as Ernest Hemingway's "a clean well-lighted space" or Virginia Woolf's "a room of one's own."

First ideas are the safer, easier fish to pull from the pond. Any preliminary ideas would work, but now there is more brain space to think of unusual ideas. "Homebrewed" could lead to recreating the look of an authentic Irish pub in the family room, including an homage to the poet Dylan Thomas.

The phrase "there's no place like home" could inspire a ruby red theme or it could lead to a *Wizard of Oz* fantasy using colorful images such as an Emerald City bedroom, a Yellow Brick Road sunroom and a "Somewhere Over the Rainbow" bathroom. Now we are cooking!

Keep pushing for new layers of connection by reviewing the words you've spilled out and the new ideas created in your head. Write everything down without censoring any ideas. Don't evaluate or critique the list until you've finished your BrainSpill session. Then, review and evaluate all of the ideas. Decide which ones make sense to put into action.

ANOTHER IDEA: SMASHING METAPHORS

This idea-generation tool uses random words in a process that I call Smashing Metaphors. It may seem hard at first, but persistence pays off and yields unusual, original thinking. The object is to force your brain to think in ways it isn't accustomed to by getting unlikely words and phrases to collide together.

Begin with three random words; close your eyes and point to three words from three random pages of a dictionary. Let the selected words trigger free association in your mind, and build on them by thinking of corresponding concepts. Write everything down as you go along. Make forced connections between the trigger words and a problem or idea you are working on in your chosen medium.

Start by free associating with the first random word (for example, *wife*). That process might yield the following words: homemaker, spouse, husband, family, woman of the house.

Now add the other two random words (in this example, *bark* and *skull*). Now it's going to get a little tough, but let's put them together for forced connections. How do the words *bark* and *skull* relate to *wife*?

Here are several examples of what we might generate:
A wife's bark might be her nagging that assaults the skull of the husband.
The dark side of a family may be the secrets that are locked away in the skulls of the siblings who look normal and happy on the outside. Or maybe bark is related to tree bark, and we begin to think of the wife as having a crusty exterior that protects her true self, like a skull protects the brain inside.

Don't worry if your ideas feel silly or the connections seem loosely tied. Let your mind roam freely wherever the trigger words prompt you to go. A free mind runs to odd and unexpected places.

This illustrates how we can push for wilder and more unusual connections to develop original ideas. When we smash together two or three random words the brain wants to find order and meaning, so the introduction of seemingly unrelated triggers supplies the juice to get the brain working harder. The brain wants to show off and surprise us, so we are frequently rewarded with fresh ideas.

This process can lead to an infinite number of creative possibilities and hours of creative fun. Practice, practice and practice some more. Make several forced connections with three random words every day. Keep your brain zany and sharp. Turn your fresh ideas into even better ideas as you put them into your stories, your music, your paintings and your poems. It can all begin with the power of words and the spark just waiting to set your brain on fire.

MY NEIGHBORHOOD CRUSADE

BY SUZANNE SIMANAITIS

IN MY NEIGHBORHOOD, DUSK ARRIVES WITH THE ICE-CREAM TRUCK. CREEPING ALONG, IT STOPPS WHEREVER CHILDREN FLAG IT DOWN WITH DOLLAR BILLS TUCKED IN THEIR FISTS. The guy who drives the ice-cream truck is a young Latino who wears T-shirts and *no habla inglés*. I hesitate calling him "the ice-cream man," as a proper ice-cream man would wear a white uniform and a hat and say things like, "Careful crossing the street, son," and, "Excellent choice, miss!" But he is the guy who drives the ice-cream truck and collects our sweaty dollar bills and hands the children their sealed-for-their-protection frozen treats.

Each evening I hear the truck coming and I hear it going. I don't say "see" because though I do see it (in all its Technicolor-decal glory,) it's the sound that makes an impression. It gets into my head and won't let go, and I'm sure I'm not the only one.

For years we enjoyed a nightly rendition of "Turkey in the Straw," a song whose name you might not recognize, but if you heard it you'd be humming along in no time. It's that kind of song. Catchy as can be, it makes you want to jump up and square dance . . . or mosey on out to buy a Rocket Pop, in this case. Gradually our perky "Turkey in the Straw" slowed and became distorted, as if it now suffered an unfortunate neurological condition and could remember its job but had to struggle to perform it. The formerly jaunty tune became painful to listen to—undoubtedly bad for business.

After months of auditory torture, the ice-cream guy invested in a new recording for the truck. I smiled when I first heard its clear tones ringing down the street. But when I recognized the new song I realized the situation had gone from bad to worse—much worse.

For, inexplicably, the ice-cream guy has chosen a music box that plays the theme from *Love Story*. From *Love Story*! Quite possibly the saddest song in the history of sad songs.

You don't even have to know the lyrics to tap into the melodrama—it's in the music. The whole thing is calculated to mess with your mind: it begins on a wistful, romantic note (young love!), which spirals slowly downward into minor chords (challenged by circumstances!) to resolve briefly into a happy key (but their love will prevail!) only to be bitterly disappointed again and again. It's a powerful song.

And here it is, rolling down my street just as evening falls. Every day. Twice on Saturdays.

It took me a couple of times to identify the tune and realize why I suddenly felt subdued after the truck went by. Every night, without eating a bite, I found myself experiencing a sensation not unlike the lethargic hopelessness that comes to one who gorges on too many frozen treats. I realized what a horrible blunder the ice-cream guy had made in selecting this song. Surely he had no idea of the awful emotional baggage it carries. It was probably on sale and he figured any twinkly music box tune would bring the kids out in droves again. How was he to know that his innocent purchase would throw the neighborhood into despair?

Or, maybe that was his devious plan all along. Maybe he works for a supersecret shadow wing of

80

the Salty Snacks Manufacturers Association seeking to discredit competitors. Perhaps this is the opening salvo in the government's war on childhood obesity. Could he be a shill for a cartel of evil dentists plotting to take forcible control of oral hygiene, and this is the first step toward their misguided sugar-free utopia?

Okay, I'm willing to concede that it was probably just one guy's lousy choice, but I'm truly concerned about this because if that song affects me this deeply, it must be wreaking total havoc on the slightly older women who populate my street. In my mind's eye I see them lounging listlessly in bathrobes, not quite able to shake off the ennui that envelops them each afternoon. I imagine my neighbor ladies bursting into spontaneous tears, one plunging after another like synchronized swimmers, from west to east as the truck trundles slowly past. The eyes well up, a single pathetic sob escapes, a valiant gulp holds back the weeping until the dam breaks and finally: surrender. A good cry is had by all, and then, one by one, they pull themselves together, blow their noses and get on with their lives, resigned to the fact that the world is a brutal place.

Meanwhile, out on the sidewalk, their kids and grandkids feel confused, their smiles fading as they slowly lose their appetites. Oh yeah, that's how insidious this song is. Even the bright-eyed children who have never seen *Love Story* can sense the change that settles uneasily over the neighborhood each time darkness falls. My heart breaks (as if it could ever be whole again!) for the children whose lives will be scarred during these brief daily encounters with the ice-cream truck. These kids are going to grow up not liking ice cream, not trusting its creamy comfort, because in the back of their minds they'll hear that sorrowful tune and recall their moms calling them to come inside now, faces stained with streaky mascara.

An entire generation of children will grow up sad, and not even a Strawberry Shortcake Bar will be able to fix it. And that makes *me* sad! I believe that ice cream is among mankind's most glorious inventions, that Fudgsicles are a work of art, and—frankly, I am unable to formulate words to adequately describe the culinary magic that is the Choco Taco.

So I've taken it upon myself to help my neighborhood reclaim its innocence, at least in terms of a God-given right to enjoy Eskimo Pies. I can't stop the ice-cream truck from terrorizing us, but maybe I can neutralize its effects with a propaganda campaign to remind everyone that ice cream is, in fact, our friend. I'd

been looking for a way to volunteer my time and skills in service to my community, but I had never found the right opportunity—or a cause about which I felt suitably passionate—until now.

My original plan was to create festively collaged postcards of vigorous, smiling people portrayed enjoying frozen treats, and send them anonymously to everyone on my street. But in this age of anthrax scares, nobody except true mail art aficionados really likes to get weird stuff in the mail, and anyway the parents would probably throw out my well-meaning artwork and the children would never reap the psychological benefits.

So Plan B is to educate the neighborhood with a series of fervently pro-ice-cream posters. Every month during an early-morning walk, I'll surreptitiously staple photocopies of the latest poster onto utility poles, between the garage sale announcements and skate-punk stickers. I have read enough about marketing to know that I'm going to have to keep putting my loving message out there for a long time to have an effect, but I'm hoping that my colorful artwork and slogans will catch people's attention and, slowly, the happy association will sink in.

It won't return the neighborhood to simpler days, when ice-cream men wore white uniforms and hats and served up sheer happiness, but it's a start.

MAIL ART TO THE SELF

JOURNALING EXERCISES TO GET YOU GOING

by Juliana Coles

PART TWO

Hello again! I hope you enjoyed creating your own version of my postcard book on page 42. We are now ready to dig deep to create content for it. Through my Expressive Visual Journaling® exercises you will learn about your self, and writing to the self heightens that experience. We are contacting something within us that has information, a source that knows far more than it usually lets on.

WHAT *IS* EXPRESSIVE VISUAL JOURNALING?

What is the difference between diaries, art journals, scrap-booking, sketchbooks, altered books, artist books and Expressive Visual Journals? Some of these terms are very specific and have their own definitions, while others can be used interchangeably. I have a unique definition for my process and use the term *Expressive Visual Journal* as the container for that process. An Expressive Visual Journal can be a blank book, sketchbook, altered book, scroll, used scrapbook, antique photo album, spiral-bound old postcards, a classical

record set, a well-traveled atlas, a worn wallet with pages stapled in, antique handkerchiefs sewn together, or any other form that might be considered or used as a book. Expressive Visual Journals come in all shapes and sizes and may be filled with rice paper, Bristol paper, watercolor paper, old ledger paper, graph paper, notebook paper, glittery paper, painted paper, whatever anyone can imagine.

What makes a book an Expressive Visual Journal is the act of combining journal writing assignments—such as non-dominant handwriting, unsent letter writing, Declarations of Independence, lists, dreams and word associations—with artmaking assignments—such as collage, drawing, painting, altered photos, rubber-stamping, totem creation and other mixed-media techniques—to create a unique book of self-expression. Extreme Visual Journalists are after the rich interior. We are concerned with our own unique inner, ancient wisdom. We want to find our voice, our style, our flair for life, by documenting our past, present and future in a book. We are *not* concerned with making art in the "pretty picture"

sense. We are not concerned with a product, or impressing an imagined audience. We want to know how to unfold, and in that moment there is remarkable beauty on the page we did not know we possessed. We do this to find out who we are and why we are here. That's what makes this Expressive Visual Journaling process so daring, risky and extreme. Only the courageous are willing to arrange this meeting with the self.

WELCOME TO THE REVOLUTION

Do not take apart your book to work on the postcards separately. The Expressive Visual Journal gains its power from the sequence of turning pages. It is through this continuous page turning that we develop a relationship with our book, thereby creating a relationship with the self.

POSTCARD ETIQUETTE

Work directly on the postcards, while they are secured in your book. The layers and textures and emergence of each piece will be far more interesting than something you plan in your head and sit down to execute, ending up with exactly what you envisioned. There are no surprises there. That's making, not creating. We create.

Pick any side-by-side set of postcards to begin. You can start at the beginning, middle or end of your book. Let your intuition take over. The left side of each spread will be for the address and postage. The right side will be the image side (but you can have writing on your image sides, and images on your address sides). Notice that for each of the following exercises you are prompted to create both sides of a postcard to or from someone in particular, but in actuality you are creating the "front" and "back" of this postcard message on facing pages in your book, not on the actual front and back of one of the postcards in the book. This process is not about the postcards, per se; it's about the journal, and it's about using mail art to create unsent letters—a powerful journaling tool made more effective in the confines of a book that can be kept safely closed and private. Begin by beginning, not thinking.

ASSIGNMENT 1:
WORLD TOUR

When you created your postcard pages, you wrote about the places you'd like to visit. Now, imagine yourself on a World Tour. It can be any era. Create a collage of this whirlwind life. Have fun, experiment and release the need to make good or acceptable art. See where spontaneity and intuition guide you. You can be "perfect" on your other projects. Address this card to the part of you that won't take the trip that you're writing about. Perhaps she's afraid, thinks she's too old or too young or doesn't have "enough" time or money. Write this part of yourself a postcard from your worldly, traveling self, an "if-only-you-knew" message from someone who knows the taste of freedom. Add labels, postage, visa stamps, etc. It's all about you.

ASSIGNMENT 2:
SPIRITUAL CORRESPONDENCE

Choose an established or imaginary god or goddess, spiritual leader, shaman, totem animal or whom- or whatever you will consult for spiritual guidance. How will you describe your journey and ask for assistance? You must realize and accept that you both deserve and require assistance.

ASSIGNMENT 3:
DIVINE INTERVENTION

On this postcard, your chosen spiritual counsel is going to write you back. Address it to your temple, monastery or sanctuary—otherwise known as your home address.

ASSIGNMENT 4:
CHINESE TOMB SWEEPING

In the spring, Chinese people visit their ancestors, sweep their tombs and bring offerings such as fruit and flowers. What ancestor's tomb would you visit (real or imaginary), what offering or gift would you bring, and how would you introduce yourself? Be attentive to that which guides and directs you—let the story unfold.

ASSIGNMENT 5:
MAP OF THE HEART

This exercise maps the grief, loss and sorrow in your heart and lets them speak. Remember, the postcard must have a writer/creator as well as a recipient. Give both characters names and treat them with honor and respect. Add advice for how to go the distance. Identify a specific disappointment from which you might never recover, and compose a picture postcard about the resulting condition of your heart. Diagram it, to be absolutely clear: "Dear so-and-so, when you left me, you took this portion of my heart with you. (See below.)"

ASSIGNMENT 6:
HOME FOR THE SOUL

Where is home and what does it mean to you? What does it house? Attach curtains and door flaps to open; add windows; expand your postcard page to include gardens or forests, a studio of your dreams, a meditation room, a chapel or a secret room.

ASSIGNMENT 7:
POSTAL ADORNMENT

Homework: Send yourself a Mail Art postcard (that's right: take it down to the post office, stick a stamp on it and slip it through the slot) and when it arrives in your mailbox at home either attach it in your Expressive Visual Journal or start a special postcard book based on ideas for projects, favorite movies, poetry, songs, anything you can think of that would be exciting to explore in a series. Populate this idea book by sending yourself more Mail Art postcards!

Mail Art is so fun because there's something exciting about a personal message being so exposed as it travels. Thanks for this opportunity to get up close and postal with you. I hope you'll mail me a postcard sometime!

POCKETS OF INSPIRATION

by Sylvia Luna / Silver Moon

What began as an art project to remind me of my favorite layering techniques surprisingly turned into something more interactive than I had first envisioned. This picturesque portfolio holds the secrets of adding layers to your artwork, thanks to the visual inspiration cards tucked inside. When you are at a standstill and do not know what to do next with your art, randomly select one of the cards to seek guidance. It works every time!

MATERIALS

- TWO 8" × 10" (20CM × 25CM) CANVAS BOARDS
- MASKING TAPE
- SCISSORS OR CRAFT KNIFE
- GESSO: BLACK AND WHITE
- SPONGE BRUSHES
- ACRYLIC PAINTS
- CRAFT STICK
- RUBBER STAMPS
- BLACK AND BROWN DYE INK PAD
- SCRAP PAPERS, EPHEMERA, TISSUE PAPER, BLACK CREPE PAPER STREAMERS
- ALEENE'S THICK DESIGNER TACKY GLUE
- EIGHT #1 COIN ENVELOPES [2¼" × 3½" (6CM × 9CM)]
- SMALL IMAGES OF PEOPLE, UP TO 2" (5CM) HIGH (FROM PHOTOS OR COLLAGE SHEETS)
- GOLDEN GLAZES IN ASPHALTUM AND RAW UMBER
- PAPER TOWELS
- COLORED PENCILS
- SCRAPS OF CARDSTOCK OR THIN CARDBOARD
- EYELETS AND EYELET-SETTING TOOLS
- SCRAPS OF RIBBON
- GEL PENS

PORTFOLIO

1. Lay the canvas boards side by side, face down on a table. Line them up along the top and bottom, leaving a ¼" (6mm) space between the boards.

2. Use masking tape to tape the two boards together, creating a folding portfolio with a tape "hinge" in the middle. Cut the excess tape flush with the top and bottom edges of the canvas boards.

3. Paint the entire front and back surface of the portfolio with black gesso. When the black gesso is dry, randomly add white gesso over some areas of the black gesso.

4. Once the white gesso is dry, paint as much of the surface as you'd like with a variety of acrylic paints, leaving some of the white gesso exposed. While the paints are still wet, scratch into the surface with a craft stick to add another layer of interest.

5. On both sides of the portfolio, stamp text or simple graphic rubber stamps using a black dye ink pad. Stamp haphazardly in all directions. Let dry.

6. Unroll a couple yards from the roll of black crepe paper streamers, and gather and scrunch it as you use Tacky Glue to tack it down along the front of the portfolio's edge. Try to avoid a fluffy ruffled look—just keep thinking "texture." Also, if you would like to display this standing up, be strategic about how you apply the gathered crepe paper along the bottom edge. Set aside the portfolio to dry.

POCKETS

1. On the back (seamed side) of each coin envelope, glue small bits of torn papers (including tissue and ephemera) to cover the envelope and overlap bits around the edges. Also collage onto both sides of each envelope flap. Do not collage onto the fronts of the coin envelopes, because these surfaces will be glued onto the portfolios.

2. Cut and glue images of people onto the embellished side of the envelopes, feeling free to let the edges of some images hang over the edges of their envelopes.

3. Dab on the Golden Glazes with a sponge brush. If the coverage turns out too heavy, wipe some off with a paper towel. Allow the glazes to dry.

4. Randomly stamp words in black and brown ink all over the envelopes. Use colored pencils to scribble all over the envelopes; try doodling or writing encrypted messages that only you can decipher.

5. Use Tacky Glue to affix the decorated coin envelopes to the inside surface of the decorated portfolio. Be careful not to glue down the envelope flaps—you want these to be able to open and close. Allow everything to dry thoroughly.

SAMPLE CARDS

1. Cut the scrap cardstock or thin cardboard into cards measuring 3¼" × 1¼" (8cm × 3cm). (They should fit easily into the coin envelopes.)

2. Demonstrate a different layering technique on each card. I featured scratching, scribbling, gesso, rubber stamps, gel pens, crepe paper, ephemera and tissue/pattern paper.
   Have fun with this step! *Remember, they're sample pieces, they don't have to be "art." Just practice the technique on the card, and then label it with the name of the tech-*nique. *Feel free to make sample cards of your own favorite layering techniques that aren't on my list. You can practice the technique on the back of each card also, or use that space to jot down notes and tips about what you've learned about that medium. Just make sure the finished cards still fit into the envelopes. Allow the cards to dry completely.*

3. Attach an eyelet to each card and embellish with ribbon to turn your cards into little tags that will fit inside the envelope pockets.

FINISHING TOUCHES

- Carry some of the imagery you used on the envelopes onto the front cover.

- With rubber stamps or found text add the words "Visual Inspiration."

- Scribble or write with gel pens and colored pencils—anywhere and everywhere!

- Wash the entire surface with a thin coat of Raw Umber Golden Glaze to unify the colors and textures.

- Finally, add small embellishments. You may also want to place tiny bits of self-adhesive hook-and-loop closure tape to help keep the envelope flaps shut (this may or may not work, depending on how you have embellished your sample cards and envelopes).

To use this "game for one," place sample cards randomly into the pockets. When you are ready to start a new canvas or you are stumped on your current project, pull out a sample card at random and explore that technique for a while. It may be just the thing your piece needed, or this small diversion into chance may get your mind working in a whole different, refreshing direction. Either way, you will not remain blocked for long!

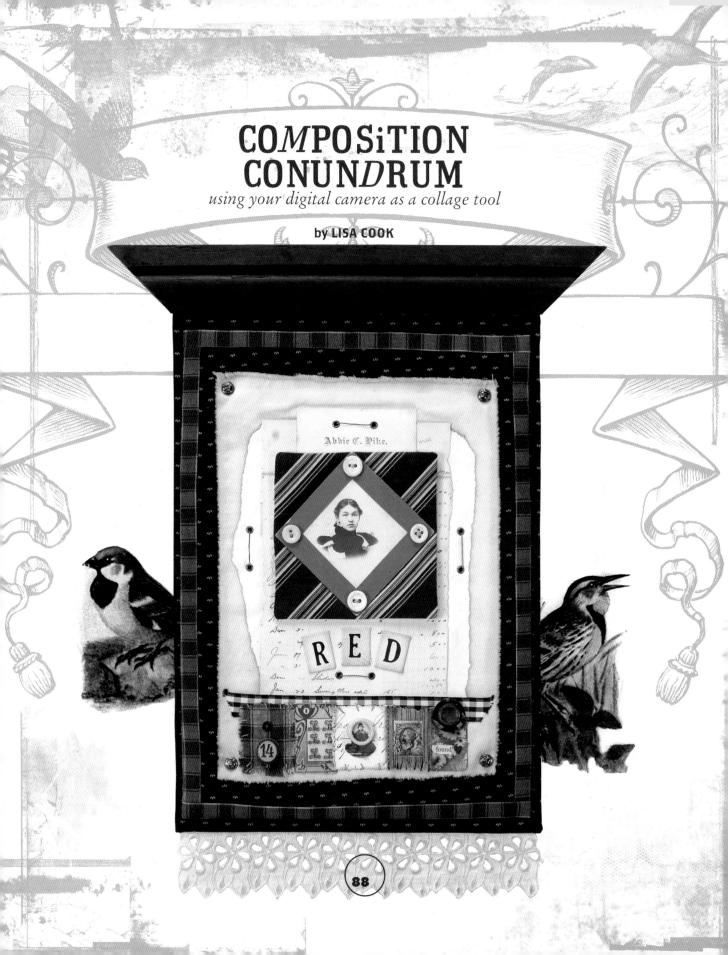

COMPOSiTION CONUNDRUM
using your digital camera as a collage tool

by LISA COOK

Abbie C. Dike.

RED

Collage artists often suffer from a composition conundrum: it is hard to decide what looks good where. You lay a few collage pieces in position and then step back to get a view from a distance. Then you try another arrangement and repeat the process again and again. Of course, it is difficult to decide which layout is the best when you can only look at one at a time, so frustration and backache settle in. One day an "aha!" moment struck when I was laying out some fabric pieces for a quilt on the floor. I could not decide which arrangement I liked best, so I took digital photos of different combinations and looked at them on my computer. Wow! I could see all my ideas in a vertical position. I could use the computer monitor like an easel and nothing was going to fall off in the process! From that moment on I took a totally different approach to composing my collage work.

Here are similar steps you can take to compose an artful arrangement for assemblage or collage.

1. Lay out the initial idea by placing the materials on a neutral background on the floor. Stand over the collage and take a picture. Add or subtract elements on the collage or move some pieces to different positions and take a few more photos. For example, a different background might look better with the same collage elements.

2. Try anything; you're exploring your options. Next, examine the artwork from a distance. Download the pictures to your computer and use a simple program like Adobe Photoshop Elements or Paint Shop Pro to size the pictures to 100–300 pixels. (Crop any distracting backgrounds.)

   Save each picture as a .jpg file and give it a simple name that helps you remember what is shown, like "RedBackWhiteButtons.jpg". Place all of the files together in one folder so they are easy to find. After you save the photos, you are ready to view them side by side to study the results.

3. Open a new Microsoft Word document, and insert each picture by using the "Insert" menu on the toolbar. Resize as necessary to fit them all on one page. Save this new document with a related title and place it in the same folder as the pictures. Choose "Print Preview" in the "File" menu to see the whole page on the screen at one time. Zoom in and out to scrutinize your ideas.

As you place the components of your artwork together keep in mind that you are dealing with basic design elements such as line, shape, texture, pattern and color. Other principles I keep in mind:

focal point
Where does your eye go to first? What pops out or what to you think should?

repetition and movement
Your eye should be carried around the picture by a repetition of design elements. A good rule of thumb is to repeat one item, such as a color, shape or pattern, three times in the collage.

balance
Are you going for a formal/symmetrical or playful/asymmetrical type of balance? Does the collage have a sense of equal weight for the sizes, colors and shapes of the pieces you are using?

contrast
A bit of surprise is always welcome to the eye and can be achieved with colors that are opposite on the color wheel, a combination of light and dark values, or another unexpected blend of elements, such as old and new.

unity and harmony
There should be a connection between the elements of the collage and a feeling of completeness. Sometimes this takes time to achieve, so save your photos, come back to them the next day and then see if you still prefer your first choice.

SAMPLE PROJECT: *SHE SEES RED*

I created a little quilt for an old photograph and decided this should be the focal point of a larger piece. I started to play with the idea of what the woman "sees." I wanted to add fabric, pieces of old ledger paper, a tag and a section of a hook-and-eye card. I took a photo and studied it. Nice balance but the dark button on the right provided too much contrast and drew the eye toward itself instead of the old photo. It had to go.

I thought I wanted to use a 7 stencil above her head—it looked good on my worktable, but when I saw it in a vertical position, I knew it was too heavy for the top. I substituted an old calling card to give the woman a name and placed some pins and eyelets on the muslin to see how they would look as an attachment idea. The repetition of red added to my theme. At first I thought the quilt would work with just the muslin background, but in the photo I could see it needed a color behind it.

I added some small items related to the red theme including a bingo marker, a postage stamp and a tiny red heart and included a piece of black checked ribbon for additional contrast. Finally I needed to find a suitable background. I took photos of several fabric selections including both red and black fabrics. The black fabric provided contrast to the muslin, but I felt it was too dark and a little dull.

I laid down another border of red underneath the black and added a piece of old lace at the bottom to repeat the muslin color. The composition had finally come together.

By framing the piece with a more elaborate border, I drew the eye into the center. I put that dark button back into the piece as it repeated the round shapes and its boldness was now balanced by the black borders.

One final but very important advantage to documenting your work as you progress is that it will be much easier to attach all the pieces to your collage or mixed-media piece because, just like a jigsaw puzzle in a box, you now have a picture to work from!

A TALE OF CAUTION FOR MODERN CHILDREN

BY CHARLOTTE KEMSLEY

Nursery rhymes are some of my all-time favorite things. Although many are sweet and fragrant, full of happiness and light, when you look a little closer some are quite brutal! They involve children being chucked out of trees, beaten up and berated, not to mention animal cruelty and eating disorders. Frighteningly, the somewhat warped humor that frequently emanates from these rhymes and tales greatly appeals to me, and I think the absurd, surreal worlds that are portrayed are a great way of expanding children's (as well as adults') mindscapes and imaginations.

Enough has been said about political correctness (or lack of it) and that is not what this project is about. It's about twisting these tales just a little bit further, creating your own deliciously weird versions. For example, I took the following well-known rhyme:

MONDAY'S CHILD IS FAIR OF FACE,

TUESDAY'S CHILD IS FULL OF GRACE,

WEDNESDAY'S CHILD IS FULL OF WOE,

THURSDAY'S CHILD HAS FAR TO GO,

FRIDAY'S CHILD IS LOVING AND GIVING,

SATURDAY'S CHILD WORKS HARD FOR ITS LIVING.

BUT THE CHILD THAT IS BORN ON THE SABBATH DAY

IS BONNY, AND BLITHE, AND GOOD, AND GAY.

… and came up with an alternative—a dig at today's world obsessed with possessions, appearance and all these other things wise beings like you and I regard with total disbelief. To create my parody version, I took the gist of each original line and pushed it to an extreme:

MONDAY'S CHILD SPENT AN INORDINATE AMOUNT ON BEAUTY PRODUCTS, CORRECTIVE SURGERY AND HAIR EXTENSIONS.

TUESDAY'S CHILD SOON BECAME STRESSED OUT FROM STAYING LATE AT THE OFFICE, AND STARTED SHOUTING AT EVERYONE ALONG WITH DRINKING TOO MUCH.

WEDNESDAY'S CHILD BECAME SELF-OBSESSED AND PUSHY IN ORDER TO STAY AT THE TOP AND WOULDN'T EVEN GIVE HERSELF A BREAK.

THURSDAY'S CHILD GOT CAUGHT UP IN THE RAT RACE TO BANKROLL HER TASTE FOR JIMMY CHOOS, BUY A PENTHOUSE FLAT AND BUILD UP A STRONG PORTFOLIO.

FRIDAY'S CHILD SPENT A FORTUNE ON COUN-SELORS AND COMPLEMENTARY THERAPIES TO MAKE THAT STRANGE PAIN GO AWAY.

SATURDAY'S CHILD ENDED UP IN REHAB WHEN THE PRESSURE OF TOO MANY BOOZY NIGHTS, UPPERS AND DOWNERS TOOK THEIR TOLL.

BUT SUNDAY'S CHILD EVENTUALLY TOOK STOCK, DECIDED TO JACK IT ALL IN AND BOUGHT A SMALL ORGANIC FARM, WRITES POETRY AND LIVES IN HARMONY WITH NATURE. AND HAD HER LITTLE TOE STITCHED BACK ON.

I liked my version so much, I decided to "publish" it as a limited edition (yeah: one!) artist book. As my base I used an 8" × 8" (20cm × 20cm) accordion-folded board book with six panels, but you can select a book that suits the twisted rhyme you come up with. If you want an accor-dion-folded board book like mine but you can't locate one, make your own by cutting apart a regular board book and reconnecting the panels with "hinges" of wide masking or duct tape.

When using cutouts from collage sheets or maga-zines, don't hesitate to really mark them up and make them your own. I scrawled lipstick on the mouths of my front cover cuties and scribbled outlines, additional details or mysterious text snippets on most of the figures inside.

Mondays child spent an inordinate amount on beauty products, corrective surgery, liposuction and hair extensions

Tuesdays child soon became STRESSED ed out from staying late at the office, started shouting at everyone and drinking too much.

get off
you
dirty
rascals

memo to: all staff

I AM THE QUEEN
OF THIS CASTLE

YOUR TURN IS
A 91

Wednesdays child became self obsessed and pushy in order to stay at the top, and wouldnt even give herself a break.

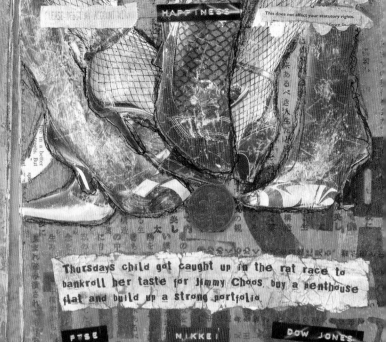

HAPPINESS

This does not affect your statutory rights.

Thursdays child got caught up in the rat race to bankroll her taste for Jimmy Choos, buy a penthouse flat and build up a strong portfolio.

FTSE   NIKKEI   DOW JONES

MATERIALS

- board book with a suitable number of panels for your rhyme
- white gesso
- acrylic paints (I used Ochre and Viridian)
- Lumiere paints (I used Sunset Gold and Metallic Olive, but choose shades in your chosen palette)
- paintbrushes
- stippling brushes
- assortment of collage images, embellishments and rubber stamps
- rub-on lettering
- adhesive foam dots
- Ranger's Distress and Archival ink pads in a range of colors
- StazOn solvent-based ink pad in black
- cardstock
- crayons, colored pencils, inks, felt-tip pens—mark-making tools of your choice
- gel medium, for gluing down images

METHOD

1. Working one side at a time, cover the entire board book with white gesso and allow it to dry.

2. Paint the book panels with acrylic paint in kind of a sloppy way to add maximum texture. When the base color is dry, sponge, dab and distress the pages with other paints (both plain and metallic) until you have a suitable background.

3. When the paint is dry, use a selection of rubber stamps and contrasting ink pads to create checkerboard or random patterns on the book panels. Don't worry about the images stamping completely—they're not meant to. You just want to create a textured background with a few vaguely identifiable bits showing up for interest.

4. I formatted my alternative nursery rhyme verses on a computer, using a grungy font. When I printed it out, rather than cutting the verses apart I tore the paper so that the edges were suitably ragged, then I crumpled and distressed the paper with ink pads.

5. For the front cover, I rubber-stamped seven little bodies on cardstock and gave them collage image heads. I used dry-transfer (rub-on) lettering to "write" the poem's new title on a series of little red tags and attached them to the book cover with sticky foam pads before running black thread through the holes to loop them all together. A couple lengths of gingham ribbon, a few wraps of black thread and a soft drink can tab complete the cover.

6. On each of the remaining pages, I added the appropriate day of the week using a mixed-up variety of large foam letter

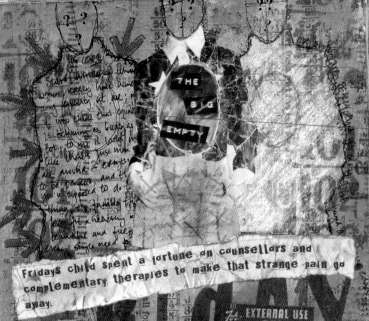

Saturdays child ended up in re-hab when the pressure of too many boozy nights, uppers and downers took their toll.

Fridays child spent a fortune on counsellors and complementary therapies to make that strange pain go away.

Sundays child eventually took stock, decided to jack it all in and bought a small organic farm, writes poetry and lives in harmony with nature. And had her little toe stitched back on.

rubber stamps. I did this roughly and messily, as some of the lettering will be covered up eventually.

7. Monday's child has holes punched in her distressed shirt, with glitzy paper scraps behind the holes. Her "hair extensions" are electrical resistors, with various stickers and doodads spelling "beautiful" around her like a halo. Further details were added using crayons, colored pencils and plain old staples (I stapled the image before I glued it to the page).

8. Tuesday's child is sitting inside a ring of time rapidly running out: rubber-stamped watches, dangerously splodged with red ink. As she's already given a pound of flesh (or more), I also added an artificial arm in the form of a silver milagro charm. Since there are bad words coming out of her mouth, a little sticker there seemed appropriate!

9. Wednesday's child is cracking the whip over her minions, all rubber-stamped images, cut out and colored. More dry-transfer lettering spells out her attitude in a "memo to all staff: I am the queen of this castle!"

10. Thursday's child is kicking money about, wearing a selection of fashionable shoes. I crumpled and gessoed the shoe images, which I cut from magazines, and I added a couple bits of Dymo lettering tape as embellishment.

11. Friday's child was created by using the central image as a template; I drew the outline of the image twice, then inserted handwritten observations on the left-hand shape and white rough crayoning on the right-hand one. Then I distressed the original cutout and glued it in the middle. Further embellishing was done with crayons, felt-tip pens, pencils and a small vintage label.

12. Saturday's child wears a dress decorated with inky splodges and an entire sheet of dry transfer lettering randomly and not very carefully rubbed onto her front. I cut the top off her head to reveal her ups and downs as symbolized by strips of measuring tape and emphasized the emptiness of her eyes with "zero" letter stickers—wow, this is depressing stuff! But I think we've hit rock bottom. Let's fast forward to:

13. Sunday's child is sitting in a fragrant garden of flowers and butterfly wings, happy at last! The central image is an actual rubber stamp that I'd unfortunately damaged by leaving a heat gun a bit too close. Rather than chucking it, I covered it with white gesso, added a few bits of acrylic paint and punched holes around the edges before threading some ribbon through.

So, there we are: *A Tale of Caution for Modern Children!* I hope you've paid attention and will take heed of the lessons learned from such hard-earned experience! Now, which nursery rhyme will you twist?

two tales most moonly

by TERRY LEE GETZ
art by CYNTHIA CARR

My husband and I have an autumnal tradition of going into downtown St. Petersburg, which overlooks Tampa Bay, to watch the full moon rise. We carry this through into October, which usually is a nicer moon because the air is drier than in September. But it was one particular September trip that got my bowels bunched.

So, we're driving down Fifth Avenue to the water and it occurs to me that our moon has no name. We call it "The Moon," but it has no proper name. All the other planets in the solar system have moons, and they all have been given proper names. I ran this through my mind and it gave me a headache. I said to Bob, "Hey, I just realized the moon doesn't have a name. That sucks." Of course, Bob said, "Yes it does. It's 'The Moon'." I hate it when he does that. I mean, obviously we call the moon "The Moon," but why, why, why does it not have its own *proper* name?

I did some research. The dictionary defines the Earth's moon as follows: 1. the only natural satellite of the Earth, being responsible (with the sun) for its tidal action or 2. any planetary satellite.

This frosted my canastas even more. The Moon has the awesome responsibility of all earthly tides, yet somewhere along the line it didn't get named. The problem with the whole "let's get pissed 'The Moon' has no name" movement is nobody seems account-able that we just passed into yet another millenium and our moon is still a nameless face in the sky.

Becoming obsessed, as I was, with the moon-naming phenomenon, I went to the Web to see if I could find what sort of lucky, named moons there are out there. They all have names! To make matters worse, they all have cool names, or certainly enigmatic names, the sort of name where you knit your brow and wonder, "Where the Sam Hill did they get that?" Sheesh—I'd settle for a goofy name at this point … any Melvin sort of name would work now, at this late

date … some old John-Doe moon name would be just as good as "The Moon."

Anyway, the Moon Name Mistress on the Web is a woman named Darbie who has composed a list of moon names broken down into Female Moon Names, Male Moon Names and Neutral Moon Names. Now, that's organization. Seeing all those moon names really brings home how much we are missing. We'll never get Adrastea, Callisto or Europa now. In fact, Jupiter has bogarted all the good moon names, in my opinion. Whoever was in charge of Jupiter moon naming was on his game; he started his day with a hearty breakfast and good coffee at Bob Evans, sharpened his pencil and said, "All right, let's name some damn moons." Mr. Jupiter-Moon-Naming Guy (you know it was a guy) wasn't bothered that Jupiter has like seventeen moons; he was ready to name 'em all—he was pumped, he was psyched, he knew his mythology. While Mr. Earth-Moon-Naming Guy (you know it was a guy) slept in late, didn't sign in on time, wasn't registered and went home to watch *Deal or No Deal* on TV instead of naming one lousy moon. The deadline lapsed for naming our moon and it won't come around again until 2030 or something. So we're stuck with Nameless Moon. I can't figure out anything that can be done about it. It's just such a shame.

Anyway, onto Tale Two. You will think I'm making this one up but I swear it's true. So, Bob and I and our dog Samson are downtown in St. Pete in September waiting for "The Moon" to come up. (This is a common problem.) It has been my understanding, from extensive reading, that the full moon rises at sunset. So, Bob looks in the paper on the appointed day and says, "The sun sets at 7:05." We bust a gussie to get downtown at 7:00, so as not to miss anything, but it's a no-show; 7:20 comes, then 7:40, and it's fully dark now, but no moon. Bob commences to say, "I think the moon is on vacation. It didn't get the memo." And I say, "I don't think the paper tells the true sunset, because it was still light out way past 7:05." Then we get into this same heated discussion of how the true sunset doesn't mean it's dark, it's the setting of the sun at a certain level in the sky or something technical that schmoes like us don't know about. We're acting like some kind of Carl Sagan wanna-bes discussing perihelion and arc and such, but to be fair, there isn't anything else to do, with "The Moon" being late and all. The fact is, "The Moon" is always late rising and so we end up on the park bench until our backsides get sore and then finally, when I am about to say, "Let's get out of here," and the dog is nodding agreement, "The Moon" comes up.

Well, it was worth the wait because September's full moon was a huge red fireball for the first twenty minutes or so. Once "The Moon" puts in its appearance, it works fast, but getting it to that point is agony. So there we are, on the bench with the dog, watching this huge red fireball of a moon rise and a woman walks by with a friend, stops, looks at us looking at "The Moon" and says, "What is *that* in the sky?" I was so shocked, I

thought maybe I was missing something, like the Space Shuttle or an alien attack, so I said, just as strangely, *"W-what do you mean?"* and she looked at me like I was nuts and said, "That big red thing in the sky. What is that?" I must have almost swallowed my tongue or had my eyes bugged out because I simply could not imagine that a middle-aged woman didn't know "The Moon" when she saw it! I mean, she was totally serious. I said, "Well, that's 'The Moon'!" and she was so embarrassed I think she gladly could have jumped into Tampa Bay, and I gladly would have helped her. She said, "Oh, my, I never thought of 'The Moon'!" which made me start wondering about stuff all over again. Like, what did she think it might be if not "The Moon"? Think on that for a while, then lie down with a cold compress and pretend "The Moon" has a name and all is right with the world.

So anyway, although we probably shall continue our moon-watching through November, it isn't the innocent pastime it seemed at first glance. I still have a bad brain cramp over it, and October's big full moon only reinforced it. There's "The Moon," all bright and beautiful, masterfully commanding tides but sadly without a proper name, and you can see how this lack of respect has led to people completely forgetting it even exists. I bet if "The Moon" was named "Sinope" that woman would remember it was in the sky, but Jupiter-Moon-Naming Guy already got that one, too. Sigh.

BAYING AT THE MOON
The moon exerts its influence over creatures

GREEK LETTERS
with modern pronunciation.

RAND McNALLY
Popular Map of
NORTHERN
STARS

Copyright by
Rand McNally & Company
Chicago
Made in U.S.A.

REINVENTION

The real voyage of discovery consists not in seek-
ing new landscapes but in having new eyes.

~Marcel Proust

If there's one thing most zine readers and zine makers have in common, it's the DIY gene. We get a rush from figuring out ways to make things work using materials we already have at hand. We're thrilled to find the broken, homeless and forlorn objects that we can transform into something useful, beautiful or meaningful.

Reinvention is a physical manifestation of imagination, with a heavy dose of recycling thrown in. Collage artists are avid recyclers. (Do you know any collage artists who can bear to throw out used gift wrap or magazines?) When an artist transforms a broken doll into the centerpiece of a cigar box shrine, that is reinvention. When an artist dismembers the doll, replaces its limbs with mossy bundles of twigs, inserts a lightbulb where the head used to be and fills the belly with birdseed, that's really reinvention! (Don't even get me started on ideas for the loose doll limbs …)

People who reinvent see the special in the ordinary. If you are among the collectors of the cruddy and the boring, your mission is to breathe new life and meaning into these rejects and wallflowers. There is another possibility hiding inside that dented can, and your challenge is to discover and release it. And it's not enough to put Thing A with Thing B. You must demonstrate relationships between the elements in order for the piece to sing.

Recycling found objects into art is appealing on so many levels. For one thing, it's cheap! Yet your creative output will be richer for following the folk-art tradition of using what

you've got. Even if "what you've got" is a bunch of neglected art supplies that you had to have yet for some reason, haven't used, reinvent them as a rewarding exercise in creative problem solving as well as frugality. I swear, one of these days I'm going to gather hundreds of my unmounted, unused rubber stamps, stitch them together into a dress, and develop a performance art piece that involves rolling around on a giant ink pad and bouncing on a canvas-covered trampoline.

My favorite reinvention projects are the ones that begin with an object that so enthusiastically launches a thought process, by the time I'm finished, the original object has been supplanted by idea after idea and it no longer even appears in the piece.

When an artist sits down to create something, it's not like turning a key and pressing down on a gas pedal. You have to navigate your way. There are choices to make, all along the path, and many of the possibilities that present themselves to you are roads you didn't even know existed before you wandered this way. Let books, zines and workshops provide you with road maps, but always remember that you can veer off the highway and tootle around on unmarked side roads whenever you feel like it.

In the spirit of reinvention, this chapter's talented contributors gather neglected mementos into artistic showpieces, alter the commonplace to suit creative needs and assign starring roles to some of your art studio's supporting players. I hope you'll follow their example and reinvent your creative self by dreaming up new possibilities for objects that inspire you, as well as a few that have confounded you so far.

artwork at left:
LOU MCCULLOCH, DONNA KOEPP, TRACI BUNKERS,
BRENDA MARKS, SONJI HUNT

MAIL ART CARDS ON THE EDGE

by TRACI BUNKERS

I feel a tingle just thinking about mail art cards. I love to make them. I love to get them. I love everything about them—the process, the oddity of found materials that go together just right, the layers and textures, and the wait to hear from the surprised recipient.

Sometimes when I make mail art cards I whip them out fairly quickly; other times I relish the hours I spend on one until it is finished. When I make them, I stand at my art table, play music and dance. It's a euphoric process for me. Although I sometimes make them without a recipient in mind, I usually make them for a specific person. They have more meaning that way. I always put myself into them fully, so that when they reach the lucky recipient (via the postal service—my messenger), they are getting a blissful part of me. A mail art card is a *gift*. And, just like other handmade gifts, they aren't always received with the enthusiasm their creator hoped for. Because of that, I have learned to be more discriminating about to whom I send my *gifts*.

While this is far from a cookie-cutter process, I can share with you some of my basics for making mail art cards that are on the edge.

As an avid recycler, I always have a stash of chipboard (in the form of cereal boxes and other packaging) waiting to be transformed into mail art. I start by cutting it with a pair of scissors into whatever shape I want. I don't worry about cutting straight or having jagged edges—the roughness is part of the charm.

I collage both sides using gel medium as adhesive. You want everything to be adhered really well since it will take an unprotected journey through the mail.

I generally cover a side with a full sheet of something for a background, maybe a map or a page torn out of a book. Then I collage on top of that. At some point in the process, I put a wash of acrylic paint over it. That helps to tie all of the different collaged pieces together and give it some harmony.

As a photographer, I literally have boxes and boxes of photographs, so I always incorporate actual photographs into my mail art cards. I almost always alter the photograph in some way, either before or after gluing it to the piece. If it's a print from a photo lab, I paint it. If it's a Polaroid, I disassemble it. I don't like it to look as if I'm just plopping photos down. The alterations help to blend the photo with the rest of the piece and add my artistic sensibility.

Sometimes I staple the edges or use brads that I smash viciously with a hammer. I feel the staples and brads supply visual and tactile interest. (And, I have to admit, for some reason I love to staple things, even if it serves no functional purpose. Staples are just cool.)

I generally work both sides of a mail art card at once, using a hair dryer to speed up the drying process. As I progress, I decide which side will have the address. Sometimes I leave a space for it and sometimes I just write or stamp it on top of whatever is already there. I keep working—painting, stamping, collaging, building up layers until I feel it's just right. I even glue on cancelled postage from other countries or stamp it with foreign cancellation stamps from the line of rubber stamps I designed. (I asked my postal clerk if this would cause any confusion, and he said no.)

Since I dance and listen to music while creating, I usually hear a line from a song that jumps out at just the right time, and I'll write or stamp it with alphabet stamps on the card. No reason—it's just fun and feels right. I work intuitively. I don't fret over what to put where, and I don't spend a lot of time digging through my stash to find just the "right" photo or piece of ephemera. I just have fun and know that I'll be happy with the end result.

Now, I must share something that, for me, makes the mail art card *rock*. I always save the little hanging flaps I find on packaging, anything with a hole in it or a plastic hook. I work these into my cards so the recipients can hang them up. Once you start looking for these hangy-things, you'll see them on all kinds of packaging.

If I am temporarily out of hangy-things, I make my own. I poke two holes in the card, and set an eyelet in each hole. Then I string a piece of wire through the holes, leaving sort of a loop between the eyelets and then wrapping the ends around the loop. You'd be surprised at what makes it through the mail. So far every hanger has made it to its intended destination, completely attached and in one piece.

Sometimes I coat my mail art cards with beeswax to make them a little more substantial as well as moisture resistant. If I decide to cover a mail art card with beeswax, I address the card first. I usually type out the address on the computer in a fun but legible font, print it out and glue it on. Then I paint a thin layer of melted beeswax on each side of the card. Sometimes I don't do a very good job of getting it on evenly, but I don't mind the rough look at all.

No matter what the orientation of your card is, landscape or portrait, put the address on with the card in the landscape (horizontal) position. If you put it on in the portrait (vertical) position, you will have to pay more postage. My cards often need extra postage anyway, because they are an odd shape, or too thick because I've glued weird, 3-D things on them. To be sure you have the right postage, take them to the post office to let them decide how much each piece needs. I always ask for the postage as stamps and not the metered strip. (After I've done all that work, the white metered-postage sticker just doesn't cut it!)

I hope this has inspired you to start making your own mail art cards. Of course you don't have to follow my process. Just loosen up, start experimenting, have fun, and see what works for you. Don't forget to dance while you are making them!

Waxing Poetic
BY BRENDA MARKS

Roses reminded Jean of the photo she sent to Earl when he was fighting in Europe.

The warm hue and matte texture lent by beeswax revives memories of a bygone era. This project incorporates woven strips of fabric encased in beeswax to create a background for an image of your choice. I've used photos of my grandma and her youngest sister, paired with fabrics that not only create a beautiful backdrop, but also remind me of the fruits of their labor at the sewing machine.

Beeswax can be found in the candle-making aisle of large craft stores. If your local farmers market includes a honey vendor, ask if they sell big bricks of beeswax. To melt it, chop it into chunks and warm it in a small, craft-dedicated Crock-Pot. When you're finished working with the melted wax, you can leave the rest of it to harden right in the pot, then remelt it the next time you want to use it. An added bonus: beeswax smells *amazing* while you're working with it.

SUPPLIES

- fabric (from an estate sale, your closet, etc.)
- scissors and/or pinking shears
- beeswax and a dedicated pot to melt it in
- substrate (wood, book board, stretched canvas, etc.)
- nonstick surface (Teflon sheet or nonstick aluminum foil)
- heat gun
- Teflon tweezers (if you plan to play with beeswax a lot, these are a great investment)
- gel medium
- photocopy (pet, first house, a sweetheart, etc.)
- acrylic paint
- paintbrushes
- attaching elements: nails, wire, screws and staples
- embellishments

PROCESS
CREATE THE BACKGROUND

1. Cut or tear fabric into strips. When deciding on the width of the strips, think about the size of your image and the level of texture you desire.

2. Dip the strips into melted beeswax. Allow excess wax to drip from the strips and set them aside on a

non-stick surface to cool. Let them cool laid flat in long strips, so they'll be easier to work with in the following steps.

3. Guesstimate the final size you will want the woven background to be. Cut one set of waxed-fabric strips to the desired width of your background. Arrange them on the substrate so that they're parallel to each other. This will be the warp of your textile.

4. Cut a second set of strips to the desired height of the background. These strips will make up the weft. One by one, weave the weft strips into the warp strips you've laid down. Start in the middle and work out toward the sides.

5. You may find it helpful to melt the strips into place as you go along. Use a heat gun to warm the wax as you weave every few strips into place; as the wax cools, the fabric strips will be joined together. Work on a nonstick surface because it is likely that some wax will drip onto the work surface, and you'll want it to lift off easily when you're finished.

6. Use the heat gun and a pair of tweezers to tweak the woven texture into the look you want. When you are happy with it, do a quick final melt with the heat gun to fuse the fabric strips together.

TRANSFER THE IMAGE

There are lots of techniques for creating image transfers from photocopies or transparencies. Here's the one that works best for me.

1. Apply several layers of gel medium to the front of a photocopied image, allowing each layer to dry completely before applying another layer.

2. Saturate the piece with water and gently rub the wet paper backing from the dried gel medium. The image will remain embedded in the thin layer of transparent plastic formed by the gel medium. Allow the transfer layer to dry.

3. Decide which side of the transfer will be the "right" side (front). Paint the image with acrylic paints on the back. It need not look perfect from the back, and it looks really cool from the front! (see photos above)

4. When the paint is dry, trim the transfer if desired, and use gel medium to adhere the painted transfer to a piece of ironed, unwaxed fabric. I used unbleached muslin for the *Alice and Jean* piece (right), but on the *Roses* piece (opposite) I just glued the transfer straight onto an unwaxed panel of yellow polkadotted fabric; the dots add a subtle and fun texture where they are visible through the transfer.

LAYER AND EMBELLISH YOUR WORK

1. Paint the substrate with acrylic paint and let dry.

2. Lay the image onto the woven background and consider your options for attaching the background and image to the substrate. When working with beeswax-covered elements, try nails, wire, screws and staples to attach the layers (glue and wax don't play well together). On *Alice and Jean* I used brass nails, supported and embellished by small washers. For *Roses* I used regular zinc washers and brass screws on the sides and decorative upholstery tacks on the front. Add embellishments to complete the piece.

ARTISTIC EXPLOSION

BY LOU McCULLOCH

An easy way to add excitement and dimension to your artwork is to make a simulated "explosion." This technique can be done over a two-dimensional work or incorporated into an assemblage or shadowbox shrine.

Begin by gluing the image you wish to show revealed from the explosion (the part that will be "burst through") onto a piece of bendable cardboard, like that from a cereal box. Here I have used a piece of vintage text. On the back of the cardboard, draw a circle or oval that will frame the image or object that will appear to be bursting through. Then draw triangular segments that reach from the center of your drawn shape to the edge, as if you were dividing it into pie slices. This does not have to be perfect; you just need enough triangular segments to provide the explosion effect. Then, use a craft knife to cut along the lines that you have drawn.

Now for the fun part: Take a pencil and roll each triangular piece around the pencil to form what will create the exploding effect. The text or imagery from the other side should show on the curled segments. Age the edges with ink pads or paints to add shadows or depth of field. This simple yet effective technique will work on items of any scale, from an artful brooch to a cigar box assemblage and beyond.

ANOTHER DIARY
OF VISUAL INSPIRATION

by SONJI HUNT

BY **SUZANNE SIMANAITIS**

A STICKY SITUATION:
THE PACKING-TAPE PURSE

I love tape. Duct tape, packing tape, printed tape, electrical tape and don't leave out good old Scotch (I mean, Scotch *tape*). Tape is, of course, good for sticking Thing A to Thing B. But it can also be the Thing itself: Yes, tape is not just for adhesive anymore; it has become an art material in its own right. Stuck to itself or to paper, tape can be formed into a sturdy fabric (that requires no sewing!) and is ready in seconds (no drying time!). Tape is cheap, plentiful and decidedly not precious, so it invites us to experiment without worrying about "wasting" anything.

Especially with paper or cardstock encased within it, a "fabric" made of layers of packing tape can be transformed into a simple yet charming purse. Try playing cards, Loteria cards or Monopoly money in your tape layers the first time, and then summon your courage and make a packing-tape purse out of some of those gorgeous little Altered Trading Cards you've collected in the past few years.

Use a solvent-based permanent ink pad to stamp images right onto naked playing cards; it'll even work on packing tape. Just add more tape on top to protect the image. Or prepare a packing-tape image transfer and slap

it on there somewhere. Seriously, the materials for this entire project cost less than five bucks, so why not go nuts and try lots of things? Spend an unpredictable afternoon making something really cute out of something unexpected.

For the "Royal Flush" purse, all you need is a deck of playing cards, a pair of scissors and a roll of good quality clear packing tape. Name brands like Scotch and Crystal Clear work best because they're sturdier and a lot more forgiving than you expect.

On your work surface, lay out an arrangement of playing cards to form the back of the purse. Lay them side by side with tiny gaps in between, where the tape can stick to itself to encase each card. When you know the approximate size and shape of your purse's back panel, set aside the cards for a moment.

Cut strips of packing tape a couple inches wider than the back panel will be and lay them, sticky side up, horizontally on your work surface. Overlap the tape strips by about ½" (12cm) as you lay them down, and use your pinky fingers to hold taut the ends of the previously laid tape strip so that you don't introduce bubbles and wrinkles as

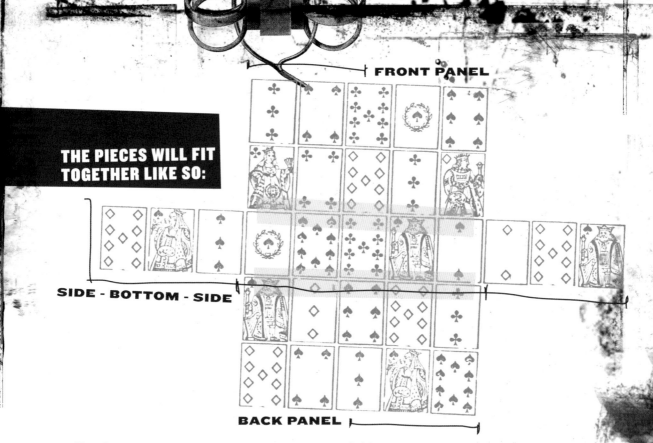

THE PIECES WILL FIT TOGETHER LIKE SO:

FRONT PANEL

SIDE - BOTTOM - SIDE

BACK PANEL

you add each new strip. I needed five slightly overlapped packing tape strips to accommodate my planned playing card arrangement.

Carefully lay the playing cards onto the tape layer the way you want them, face up. When they're all in place, flip the whole piece over and use your fingers to burnish the tape onto the card backs, which will appear on the inside of the purse. If you have a few wrinkles or bubbles it's no big deal, but if it's really bugging you, carefully peel the card from the tape to reposition it. It's not easy, but it's not impossible.

Flip the piece over so you're looking at the outside again. Add some decorative details (I used printed tape and hearts cut out of red painters tape) and then lay more horizontal strips of packing tape to cover the whole thing, slightly overlapping each strip as before. Burnish the tape well to ensure good contact and the clearest possible appearance.

With scissors, trim the excess tape about 1" (3cm) outside the edge of the card arrangement. Now do the same thing (only maybe a little more neatly, please) to create the front of your purse. The front and back purse panels should be identical in size and shape.

Make the sides and bottom panel of the purse as one long strip. The bottom panel will be however many cards wide your front and back panels are, and you'll need enough cards in the side panels to come up the whole

height of the front and back panels. If you are using standard playing cards, you should find that the height of two vertically laid cards equals the height of three horizontally laid cards.

So for my purse that is five cards wide, I needed a side-bottom-side strip of eleven cards (three for one side, five for the bottom, and three for the other side).

Create the side-bottom-side strip the same way you made the front and back panels: lay down long strips of packing tape, arrange the cards face up on the tape, then lay more tape on top to encase the cards. Trim the strip about 1" (3cm) from the edges of the cards. Make snips in the excess tape where the sides meet the bottom, so that you can miter the tape at the corners of the purse.

Tape the card panels and long strip together to form a boxlike shape (see diagram, this page). You'll need to use lots of packing tape and cut little flaps and darts—you'll see where they're needed as you go along. First lay strips of tape to attach the front and back panels where they belong at the center

ANGELS ON MY SHOULDER PURSE

To add strength to the integrated shoulder strap, I laid the Angel cards onto a layer of duct tape rather than packing tape. Strips of duct tape line the entire length of the strap.

KEEP ADDING EMBELLISHMENTS

Keep adding embellishments under layers of clear packing tape until you are satisfied. Cut the tape cleanly with scissors instead of relying on the built-in cutter, so it'll lay flatter and look nicer.

Now all you need is a handle, and you have lots of options here. I enlarged the back of a playing card on a color copier, printed it onto cardstock, cut the copied "cards" into a general handle shape and decorated the plain backs with more fancy tape. When the handle shapes are cut out, encase them in strips of packing tape, cut them out again, then wrap short pieces of packing tape the whole way around each part of the handle so the layers of cardstock, tape and packing tape do not delaminate from each other.

How to attach the handles to the purse? Um, how about using tape?! Burnish it into contact with the purse and handles especially well. Reinforce the connection by installing brads or eyelets, if you wish.

If you'd like a shoulder strap for your purse, set a couple big eyelets at the top edge of each side panel and tie on a length of wide ribbon or fancy ropelike upholstery trim. Or you can make your side-bottom-side strip of playing cards really long so that it extends past the top of the purse and meets itself to form a shoulder strap, like I did on the "Angels on My Shoulder" purse.

That's what is so very fun about this project: once you get the hang of working with tape, the possibilities are endless. Vary the materials: use duct tape strips for the inside surface instead of clear packing tape, or collage torn papers together instead of using playing cards. Play with the shape: round the corners into a big oval for a lozenge-shaped bag, or build a taller back panel that folds down over the front to form a purse flap, or make one big panel with eyelets along the sides and fold and whipstitch it into a clutch purse.

Clear packing tape can provide a ton of fun, as can plain gray duct tape, but if you scout around the hardware store, office supply store and gift wrap boutique you'll discover a rainbow of interesting tapes to play with. Push it beyond the expected and surprise yourself with your ingenuity.

of the side-bottom-side strip, then fold the edges to meet and tape each seam with one strip of packing tape on the outside and another strip on the inside. Reinforce all the edges (inside and out) with more strips of tape, mitering wherever necessary.

When the side seams are all taped up, add more embellishments. Trim around the edge of the purse opening to neaten things up and run a piece of tape around the entire rim, adhering one edge of the tape on the outside of the purse and folding the other edge of the tape to the inside of the purse. I used red painters tape for this step, so to secure and seal the red tape I laid a strip of clear packing tape over it. The red tape would fall off quickly if left to its own devices.

Throughout this project, don't worry about using too much tape. Just lay it on as smoothly as you can and burnish it as you go. Additional layers will add strength to the purse and, hey, you've probably got a hundred yards of the stuff on that roll, so go nuts with it if you want to.

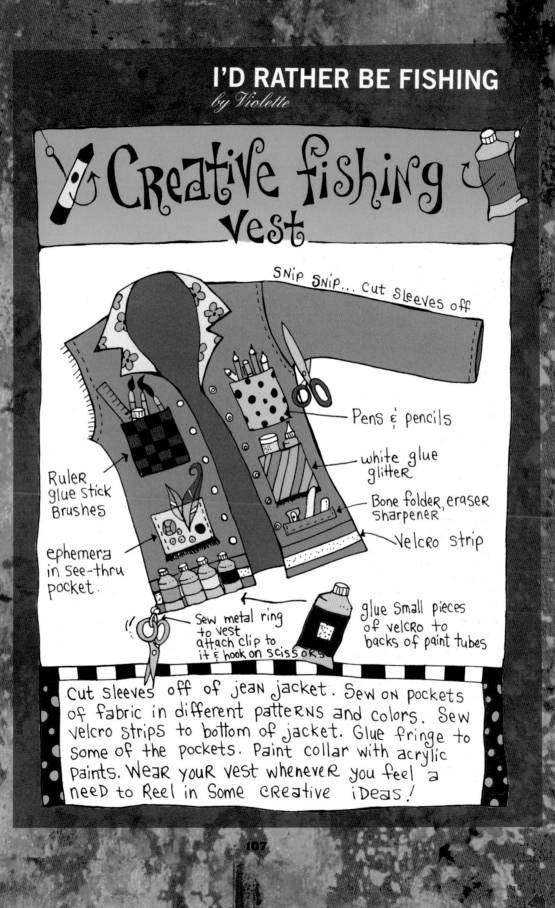

Creative fishing Vest

SNIP SNIP... cut sleeves off

Pens & pencils

white glue
glitter

Bone folder, eraser
sharpener

Velcro strip

Ruler
glue stick
Brushes

ephemera
in see-thru
pocket.

Sew metal ring
to vest
attach clip to
it & hook on scissors

glue small pieces
of velcro to
backs of paint tubes

Cut sleeves off of jean jacket. Sew on pockets of fabric in different patterns and colors. Sew velcro strips to bottom of jacket. Glue fringe to some of the pockets. Paint collar with acrylic paints. Wear your vest whenever you feel a need to reel in some creative ideas!

THE THROAT TOTE

by *Elizabeth Dunn*

SUPPLIES

- thick cardstock (such as a manila folder)
- scissors
- craft knife
- ruler
- awl
- paper ephemera
- gel medium
- yarn, ribbon or raffia (for a lightweight yet sturdy neck strap)
- beads, dangles or charms
- self-adhesive hook-and-loop tape (Velcro)
- Optional: decorative scissors, fabric

I designed this little tote—big enough for a lipstick, some cash, a house key and much more—as a tiny purse for a night on the town. But when my friend Suz saw one she instantly thought of it as a reliquary, an enclosure for special little treasures. When you make one (or two!) you can deck it out to express your unique fashion sense and use it like an amulet to gather the symbols that empower you as an artist: a milagro, a feather, a crayon of your favorite color—whatever beckoning talisman the muse lays in your path today.

This project is simple, although accurate measurements are a must. Follow the provided diagram on the opposite page and you'll do fine! Although thicker cardboard or mat board would be sturdier, I suggest starting with thick cardstock (my favorite is manila folder material—it's very easy to work with).

The width of the box can be widened by equally increasing the width of all panels labeled "B" on the template (see the designated arrows on all five "B" panels). As long as all "B" panels are the same width, the box will fold and fit together properly.

THE FOUNDATION

Cut out and score cardstock according to the template. To score, I use my craft knife and apply slight pressure (not enough to cut all the way through) as I glide it across the cardstock's surface, using a ruler as my guide. A bone folder works, too.

Cut edges of D1 and D2 (see "D" markings) to separate those tabs from the bottom "B" panels. Using an awl, poke small holes for the straps where indicated.

THE OBSERVATION

Before collaging, bend the cardstock along the scored lines and see how the panels fall into place to create the box shape. For instance, take note of how the front flap is "upside down" relative to the rest of the panels (thus the direction of how those images are glued down will differ), and how the front flap covers up a portion of one of the panels when the box is closed. Also, note which panels will be *hidden* when the box is glued together and thus will not require decorating.

THE SKIN

Flatten the cutout shape and begin collaging, gluing down paper images and scraps onto the surface using gel medium. Feel free to cover up the scored edges (in essence, wrapping images from one side of the box onto another).

Don't hesitate to pile a lot of collage layers onto this baby. The added thickness will make the box sturdier. It's a great way to use up lots of the little scraps you've accumulated! (Yes, we know all about you and your scraps problem.)

At any time, you can spot-check how the box is coming together. But before bending the box, you must *rescore* any collaged-over scored edges to ensure clean breaks.

If desired, you may cut the front flap a little shorter to expose more of the underlying panel (A), but *don't cut the front flap narrower than the width of the box* (B). Flatten and continue collaging until you are happy with the result.

For a more finished-looking tote, you can glue fabric to the inside surface of six of the box panels (see photo). Be sure not to apply fabric to *hidden* panels that will be glued to each other to form the box structure.

Before gluing the box together, *repuncture* the strap holes carefully while the cardstock can still lay flat.

THE ASSEMBLY

Apply a thin layer of gel medium on all four *hidden* panels and glue the box together. While holding the box together, sit it upright on a hard surface, lift up the front flap and place an object inside that will apply pressure to the bottom (a closed ink pad or a deck of cards works well). Hold everything in place for a minute so the gel medium can set, then allow the box to dry.

Seal the outside of the box with a thin coat of gel medium and set aside to dry. Determine what type of strap you want (ribbon, braided yarn, etc.) and the preferred length. Tie one end of the strap through a side hole (with the knot inside the box).

Add beads, dangles or charms, then insert the other end of the strap through the hole on the opposite side of the box and tie a knot inside the box to secure it. Dab some gel medium on each knot for extra reinforcement.

Cut a small piece of hook-and-loop tape that is no more that ¼" ¼" (6mm 6mm), remove the backing paper from each side, and adhere it to secure the underside of the front flap to the front panel. Now tuck some tiny treasures into your tote, and wear it with pride.

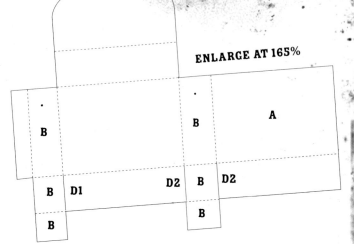

ENLARGE AT 165%

FOLDABLE
memories

Text by SUZANNE SIMANAITIS
Artwork by ELSIE SAMPSON

Some people say that memories are slippery, but I think they're more like origami. The brain has the same material to work with every time you revisit a memory, but your recollection is not always picture-perfect. You might remember only one side of a conversation, or maybe the beginning and ending have been folded toward the middle with corners flipped back on itself, until it only vaguely resembles the original. Perhaps an event that, at the time, seemed fairly flat and straightforward becomes, in memory, a many-layered and convoluted version of itself, with new contours you hardly recognize.

This "Foldable Memories" project gives physical expression to this trick of memory. A few simple folds and some strategically placed adhesive allow you to build a small collage that can be folded, flipped and rearranged into juxtapositions that you didn't expect, yet which somehow ring true.

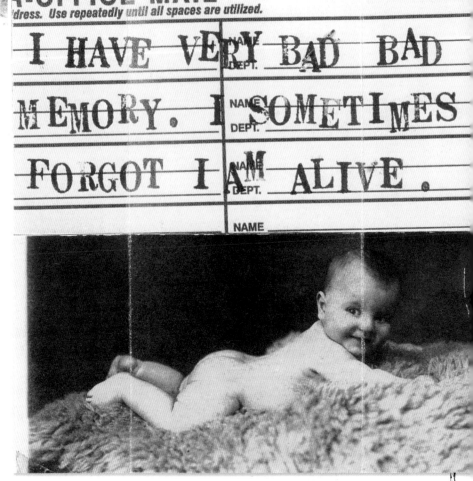

GIVE THIS A TRY

All the materials you need are probably at hand: some glue, a few index cards, scraps of ephemera and a pencil so you can leave your mark. You'll be surprised by the elegance and eloquence of this simple form.

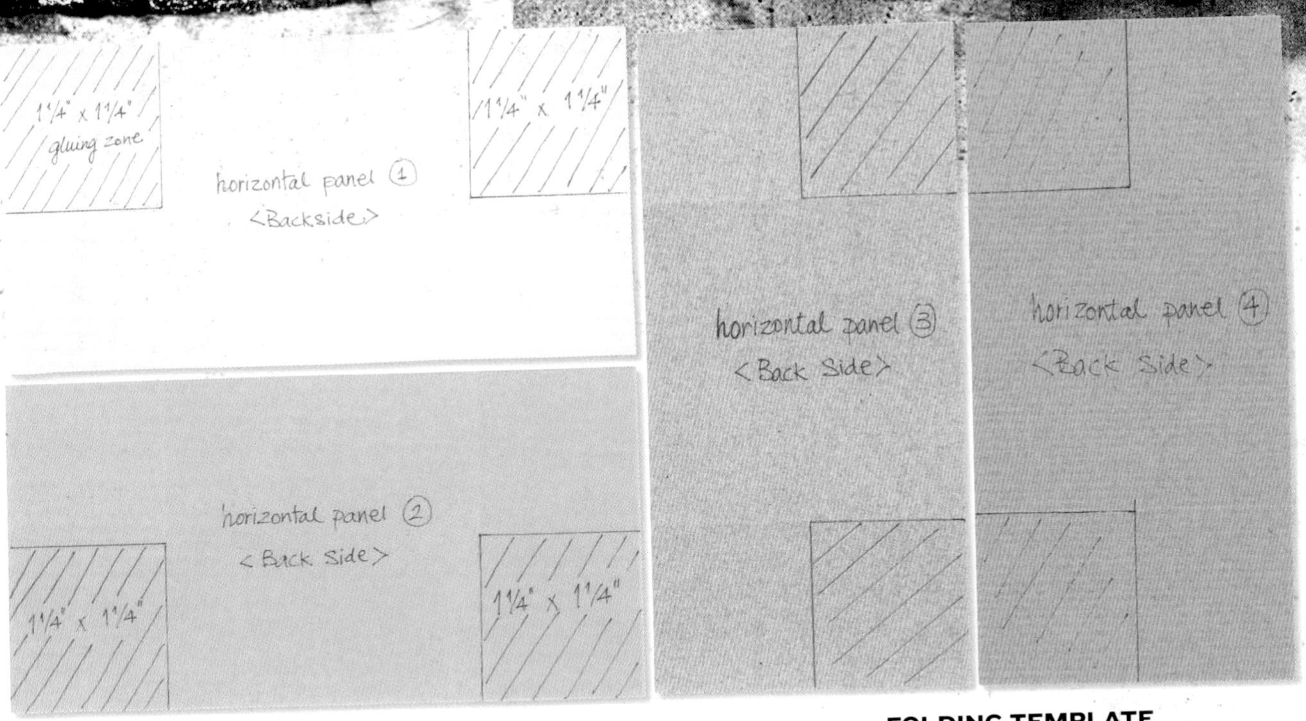

1¼" x 1¼"
gluing zone

horizontal panel ①
<Backside>

1¼" x 1¼"

horizontal panel ③
<Back Side>

horizontal panel ④
<Back Side>

horizontal panel ②
<Back Side>

1¼" x 1¼"

1¼" x 1¼"

FOLDING TEMPLATE

Use this template as a guide to create your own folded memory.

REMEMBER...

The cool thing about this project is that the finished piece can be folded to stand in two different ways, one of which is shown here.

A BOOK OF MEMORIES

BY CHRISTINE COX

All my life, I've been a pack rat of the first order. I come by it honestly; most of my relatives have the same affliction. Recently I dug out a treasure trove of old correspondence: poems written for me, drawings, greeting cards, photos—an embarrassingly rich mine of creative ore. I had a ball going through the folders of goodies and couldn't bear the thought of putting them all back into their dark, lonely hideaway. I wanted to display the items but I also wanted to respect their age and character.

I developed the following project to deal with all the cards. Being a bookbinder, it was a natural choice for me to bind the cards into books. Chronology was a problem so I decided to organize the cards by size and color instead. While the handmade cards tended to be made with durable cardstock and handmade paper, most of the purchased cards were made of thinner paper —unsuitable for sewing into a book without extra support.

I made one giant book from 138 handmade cards. It looks great opened all the way up and wrapped around a vase or candle, fanned out like a star. Because this book was so big, I started with three yards of thread for each paired station, but as I sewed I used a "weaver's knot" to add new lengths of thread as needed (see page 114).

My favorite binding stitch for these books is the chain or Coptic stitch, one of the oldest binding stitches known. It's fun to vary the thread colors or even to switch colors part way through sewing. My Christmas card book has red and white alternating thread and red paper guards on every other card spine. I call that book *Candy Cane* in honor of its sweet colors.

When sewing a chain stitch, you must use even tension and form each stitch the same way every time, otherwise the spine will not look tidy. I tend to do each step on each piece of thread from left to right, every time. This consistency makes the stitches uniform throughout the entire sewing of the book.

In the instructions below, the stitching holes will always keep their original numbers (Hole 1 is always the far-left hole, and it isn't going anywhere) but because the threads and needles switch places frequently during the stitching process, when I say Needle 1, I mean whichever needle is on the far left. Then, from left to right, the remaining needles are Needle 2, Needle 3 and Needle 4. To state it another way, each needle will be identified by the same number as the hole from which it most recently emerged. Don't get confused that Needle 2 was called Needle 1 on the last row of stitching—that doesn't matter. Trust me, when you get into the rhythm of this stitch, it'll feel easy and natural.

TOOLS & MATERIALS
- *greeting cards*
- *piece of paper*
- *pen*
- *ruler*
- *awl*
- *hole punching cradle*
- *4 large eye, blunt needles*
- *2 pieces of four-ply waxed binder's thread [each piece 1 yard (1m) long, and more thread standing by if necessary]*

TECHNIQUE
1. Sort the cards by size, color, event, chronology or however you see fit. Try arranging them a few different ways to see what appeals to you. The simplest books are those made from cards that are similar in height and width. Also, remember that whatever card is on top of the pile will be the front of your book. Choose one that will make a good-looking cover. Eliminate any cards that are made from paper that will not stand up to sewing or those that have spines or structures unsuitable for sewing, such as pop-ups or other elements that might be in the way. Wildly different sized cards create design challenges, and those can be fun, but for your first venture it may be wise to work with cards of similar size.
2. Create a hole-punching template by cutting a piece of scratch paper to the same height and width as the *largest* card. Fold the paper in half (in the same direction as the cards) to mark the center. Now unfold the template and draw four dots on the fold line indicating where you want to put the stitching holes. These holes should be between the top and bottom of the *smallest* card in your book.
3. Mark one side of the template B (bottom edge).
4. Use an awl to poke holes in each card, with the template as a guide. I like to use a hole-punching cradle for this. You simply set the cradle lengthwise

in front of you and lay three or four nested cards into it. Lay the template inside the top card and jog everything up to the right-hand side of the cradle. This alignment up against the leg of the cradle is critical. It ensures that all the cards will line up at the bottom and your book will sit correctly on the shelf. Use the awl to poke a hole wherever there is a dot on your template. Keep poking holes until all the cards are done. Un-nest the cards, check their orientation and set them in a pile, face up, on the table in front of you.

5. On each of the two pieces of binder's thread, thread two needles—one at each end.
6. Make the tails at either end of the thread the same length. This will help you find the center of the thread when you start sewing.
7. Place the first card (the front of your book) face down on a flat surface with the spine edge toward you. Try to keep the book lying in place on the table the entire time you're stitching. It may seem awkward at first, but it will help you keep your stitches tight and even.
8. Open the card (which will now be called Card 1) and starting from inside the card, feed one needle (Needle 1) out of the far left hole (Hole 1). Feed the needle on the other end of the same piece of thread (Needle 2) out of the next hole (Hole 2). Pull the needles through the holes evenly so that the section of thread between the holes is the exact center of the thread. Now do the same procedure in the two right-hand holes (Holes 3 and 4) with the other piece of thread and Needles 3 and 4.
9. Place the next card (Card 2) on top of Card 1. Align them at the bottom and be sure that the spine edges of the cards line up precisely. During the entire stitching process, work at keeping the spine edges aligned and the tails (bottoms) of the cards even. (The top of the book may not align because the cards may be of different heights.) The more movement and lack of alignment you have, the looser the finished book will be.
10. Pick up Needle 1 (remember, this means whatever needle is at the far left and just came out of Card 1/Hole 1) and put it into Hole 1 in Card 2, stitching from the outside to the inside. Repeat with each of the other three

needles—the needles are just going *into* the holes in Card 2 directly above wherever they came *out of* Card 1.

11. Working inside Card 2, cross Threads 1 and 2 and then send what is now the new Needle 1 out Hole 1. Send the new Needle 2 out Hole 2. Repeat with Needles 3 and 4.

12. Add Card 3 to the top of the stack and then bring each needle into each hole directly above where it came out of Card 2 (from the outside to the inside). Just like in step 10, you're simply stitching straight up into the new top card.

13. Cross the threads as you did in step 11, and send each needle out its new hole.

14. Now you will make your first link stitch. These are the stitches that bind one card to the next and form the attractive chain across the spine of the finished book (see photos on page 112). Look at the thread attached to Needle 1 and Needle 2, going through Hole 1 and Hole 2 adjacent to each other on Card 1. These two holes are commonly known as a "paired station." Holes 3 and 4 are your other paired station on this project. Link stitches are made by swinging each needle to the outside of the paired station (that is, Needle 1 will swing to the left of Hole 1 while Needle 2 swings to the right of Hole 2) and then ending

with each needle pulling its thread in between the holes of that paired station (see diagram on page 115). Here's what I mean: Without moving the stack of cards from their place on the table, lift the top two cards a little. Send Needle 1 between Card 1 and Card 2, around the knot and then back out to the outside of the spine. Send Needle 2 between Card 1 and Card 2, around the thread that spans these two cards at Hole 2. When you've completed this maneuver with all four needles, at each end of the stack you should have a pair of holes with two threaded needles hanging in between them.

15. Pull each thread reasonably tight. This tension is important. You want the link to be tight because it's part of the integrity of the sewing, but if you pull it too tight, the chain stitches won't be well defined and pretty. When each thread is tight, add another card to the top of the pile and then put each needle into the corresponding hole in the new card (Needle 1/Hole 1, Needle 2/Hole 2, etc.).

16. Cross the threads as you did in step 11, and send the needles back out their respective holes.

17. Now you will do another link stitch. As before, just lift the top 2 cards when sending the needles around the existing stitches.

18. Continue sewing in this manner until you run out of cards.

19. After making the link stitches that attach the final card, send the needles back inside the final card and then tie each pair of threads (really the two ends of a single thread) into an overhand knot to finish. Cut each thread to about ½" (1cm) and then twist the ends to unply the thread. This helps prevent the thread from untying itself and makes it lay flatter inside the book.

HOW TO TIE A WEAVER'S KNOT

While stitching a book together, you may get to the end of the threads before you are finished. Don't worry—it's easy to attach another length of thread using a Weaver's Knot:

Step 1
On the inside of a card make two loops in the old piece of thread. Note in the drawing where the thread falls in front and where it falls behind.

Step 2
Bring the right loop up through the left loop from behind.

Step 3
Pull the thread end coming from what was previously the left loop and tighten just that loop.

Step 4
Insert the new piece of thread into the remaining loop (formerly the right loop) and pull everything tight. Trim the old thread to about ½" (1cm) and separate the plies of thread to make it harder for the knot to come undone.

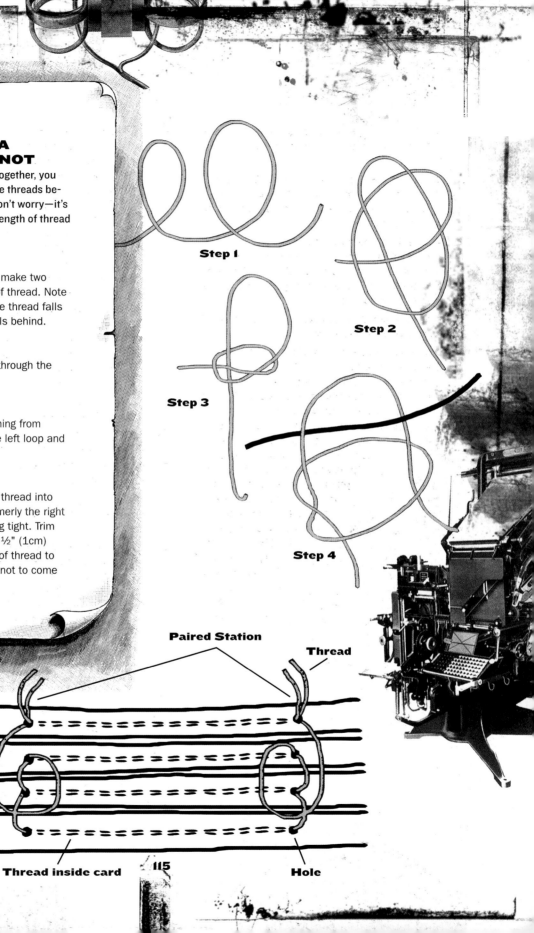

Step 1

Step 2

Step 3

Step 4

Paired Station

Thread

Card 4

Card 3

Card 2

Card 1

Thread inside card

Hole

treate hope believ

WHY CAN'T
YOU BEHAVE?

Street Games of Boys in Brooklyn, N.Y.
By Stewart Culin
American Journal of Folklore 4 – 1891

The games of which I shall give an account are all boys' games or
games in which both boys and girls participate, and were all described
to me by a lad of ten years, residing in the city of Brooklyn, N. Y., a

The tulips are too excitable
— SYLVIA PLATH

March

May

July

September

OBSTACLES

FORGET SAFETY. LIVE WHERE YOU
FEAR TO LIVE. DESTROY YOUR
REPUTATION. BE NOTORIOUS.
~RUMI

Genuine fear is a primitive survival instinct. It heightens your awareness because you might need to react at a moment's notice. This is not necessarily a bad thing. The problem is that fear focuses on the worst-case scenario, ignoring any chance of creating a more positive outcome.

If you never feel afraid, you probably aren't exploring the full possibility of your life. Facing new fears means that you are trying new things, things you might never have dreamed of. But facing the same old fear over and over again is stagnation, and stagnant stuff stinks. Ask yourself whether this fear is protecting you or restricting you.

Fear is a devious foe for a fertile mind because it is imagination turned against itself. All the fears you dream up—it's not good enough, the audience won't understand it, it'll never sell—seem valid thanks to your Oscar-worthy overachievement in creative thinking, but, in fact, they are usually just excuses, misguided attempts to avoid risking personal and artistic growth.

When you examine the fears that are holding you back, you will probably find that they have more to do with what other people might think about your work than about what you think about it. Once you realize that, you must set aside those concerns and draw the picture, write the poem, create the collage. Do it with your full attention on the doing. Trust your gut and listen to your materials. It's your job to make the art you're meant to make, to probe the corners of your comfort zone.

Fear can be useful. Your examination of what is really bugging you can be the friction that provides a spark of inspiration. Although it was only one contributing factor among many, my friend Helga Strauss and I launched ARTitude Zine partly as a way around the fear of sending our artwork to other publications. "We'll show them, we'll publish it ourselves!" we laughed, taking back the power and defusing the potentially embarrassing disappointment of our work being turned down (which, in retrospect, we would have managed to live through anyway). A trusted friend will often turn out to be your greatest ally in facing fears. They give it to you straight—real options—rather than the distorted faux-future of your overactive imagination.

Our greatest reward in creating ARTitude Zine was that it became a platform where others could take steps toward facing their own fears. Our creative act turned out to be a catalyst for others to summon their courage, and it became a continuum, a circle of brave creative acts that any number of us can draw inspiration from or contribute to at any time.

That's not to say that we are now fearless. Far from it. With every new success there may come a new fear—as in, top that! Maybe you fear the unknown. Maybe you fear conflict. Fear is why you procrastinate. Fear is why you feel blocked. When you experience fear, keep the channel open. Don't judge the creative output as it comes, just do it. Honor your instincts and keep going. Do not compare your work to others' and do not anticipate what people might say about it. Let them form their own opinions—and they will—and you will usually find that they are far more understanding and more supportive than you expected. When you befriend fear's uneasy energy, you begin to understand it, and you can use that knowledge to move forward.

artwork at left:
JULIE SADLER, SARAH FISHBURN, JILL JONES,
JULIANA COLES, MARY HALDEMEN, SUZANNE SIMANAITIS

THAT VOICE INSIDE YOUR HEAD

by Cheryl Reed, PhD

art by Melissa McCobb Hubbell and Julie Sadler

Check the calendar: it's Take a Witch out for a Latte Week! This is a much neglected practice, one that's due for some good PR, because I'm afraid that creative types are more likely to give her a boot in the behind and lock her in a dark closet.

When I say "witch" I'm not talking about the nature-loving, scrupulously vegan naturopath who will brew you a nice cup of herb tea and read your tarot cards. No, I'm talking about that green-faced, curiously dressed, bitter woman who cackles at inappropriate times and shrieks humiliating things in your face, usually when you're feeling the most vulnerable. The one you'd like to forget is inside your head. *That's* the one to take to Starbucks. Be sure to bring a notebook and something to write with, because she'll have a lot to say. (Doesn't she always?)

"What?" you say? "*What?* After all the energy I've spent trying to melt her into a puddle of goo … deactivate her broom … trick her into transforming into mentorish Internal Editor or severe but savvy Art Critic? Take *her* out so she can embarrass me in public? *I don't think so!*" Well, here's the thing. That attitude kind of ticks her off. She's a witch and she's good at what she does. She takes her job seriously and she, like all of us, wants some acknowledgment that she's astonishingly amazing. Can you blame her? Buy her one of those little pastries while you're at it.

Think about it this way: the energy you expend trying to control her could really pump up your own creative work. And if you can convince her to lend you some of *her* energy … well, you can see the potential. You'll probably never be schmoozy friends. Yours will always be a relationship built on a sort of dreadful respect. But this is one character you want on *your* side. See?

Besides, there's a little spell you can use to divert that energy that's zapping all over the place right into your work. Interested? It's just one word, and the beauty of it is that it's a common word that everyone uses rather carelessly, so no one will know you've just pulled out a really crafty tool. Your victory will appear effortless and earn you all kinds of respect. The trick (and there's always a trick) is in *how you energize it* and *where you point it*. Once you get the hang of it, well—look out. So, are you ready? Here's the magic word:

nevertheless!

Told you it was simple. If that's too pedestrian for you, try it out in different languages. Italian: *Nonostante!* Or maybe Latin: *Nihilominus!* Japanese is short and crisp for use in emergencies: *Demo!* Try out several variations and find one your mouth feels good about, because you want it to slip out without warning when you need it. *Voilà!*

THE LATTE BLOG

My client (screen name: ArtForce1) is writing a novel, the kind you buy so you can keep it on your shelf and read it again and again. The kind Hollywood turns into movies starring Olympia Dukakis or Meryl Streep. She's also a really cool painter and art teacher (her work actually hangs on the walls of the places she takes her witch out to for lattes). But lately, her book project seems stuck in neutral. She's hearing a cackle in her head. I'm her creativity coach (screen name: FairyCoachMother), and we have ways of dealing with that …

ArtForce1: I have periodic lapses in confidence that manifest as ugly voices in my head. The Wicked Witch may make an appearance if I start to get somewhere with this novel. I'm sure you've met her. Merciless woman. I've spent years trying to get her to shut up and she still comes through, like a radio transmission full of annoying static.

FairyCoachMother: Next time the witch shows up, listen to her! She has something to tell you. She gets your attention by driving you crazy. Really, she's part of you that wants good things for you but she's a little challenged in the communications department. She has a crummy job: making you feel rotten so you have to make choices, map boundaries, and turn your experiences into energy for doing what you came to earth to do.

ArtForce1: My witch calls on the abandoned little girl inside me and tries to make her feel sorry for herself—to convince herself she doesn't deserve good things. My neurotic adult self believes it.

FairyCoachMother: I know Witchy Woman acts out, but she had a challenging childhood (yours!) and it changed her, somehow. She became shrill and bitter and really doesn't know how to tell you

she loves you very much, and desperately wants your attention so she can help you. So turn your energy, and hers, to the same focus. Take her to your favorite coffeehouse and have a nice heart-to-heart. She'll be so impressed by your kindness. Also, she finds it harder to nag with hot liquid in her mouth.

These voices inside our heads have a job to do and part of it is to make us certain about who we are and what we're about. And we all have them! And they have such power over us! And they make such great art when we can use their magic to animate our visions!

Melissa McCobb Hubbell

ArtForce1: I love your ideas about how to deal with the witch. She really is functionally important, and I forget that because so much associated with her realm is surrounded by shame and sadness. I lose sight of the fact that she has something of value to contribute.

FairyCoachMother: I'll tell you a little secret about your witch: since she operates on a magical plane, you can use magic to capture her power for yourself. Here's a magic word: *Nevertheless.* Yes, I know, it seems innocuous, but that's because the International Witches and Saboteurs Union requires that it be in disguise. It's a very powerful incantation. Here's how it works. She says, "You'll never finish this book," and you say, "*Nevertheless*, that's what I'm working on today." She says, "No one wants to hear from you! You're exposing yourself and this will only lead to tears!" and you say, "*Nevertheless*, I'm writing the stories I hear inside." You can see where I'm going with this.

ArtForce1: Nevertheless . . . an extremely good idea. I can see immediately that it will work for me. It appeals to another part of the little girl who believed deeply in magic, and is now an adult who is just as sure that things I cannot see do exist.

A few weeks later …

ArtForce1: Saturday in my studio, nothing seemed to work. Got distracted by the kids' sculpting class down the hall, didn't like any of my own ideas, and just couldn't get focused. Got nothing done, nothing, nothing! I'm distracted by life—a parent's visit, an argument with someone I care about. And after a time of having my book's characters practically jump in bed with me, they currently seem uninteresting and blah. The witch was back in full force: just who do you think you are, writing this book? You tried it before; why did you think it would work this time?

FairyCoachMother: And you replied … ?

ArtForce1: I'm not doing too well with *Nevertheless*. Everything's frustrating me right now. I gave up my tickets to a ballgame I really wanted to attend, and then felt cheated. Tried to spend the evening writing but that went nowhere. Silly, I know. I keep trying to tell myself it shouldn't matter. . . But it does!

FairyCoachMother: I think we try to talk ourselves out of certain feelings we have ("This shouldn't be bothering me so much") but in actuality we need to acknowledge exactly how we feel. Whether they're about a book or a ballgame, our feelings are important because our psyches make them important. If we could "think" them away, I would agree that they're "silly" or unimportant. But the very depth of the feelings signals to me that your psyche is trying to get your attention.

Later …

FairyCoachMother: I read what you sent me, and I LOVE YOUR WORK! It's lyrical and sensual. It draws you right in, feels like those words were searching for each other all their lives and blissfully found each other at last. I immediately cared about these characters. I think this will be a wonderful book and I absolutely think you should continue the process you've started, because it's obviously working.

Still later ...

ArtForce1: Having trouble writing and thinking about writing lately, but it's nice that "lately" is only the last two days or so, whereas once upon a time that meant months at a clip. I just feel blah and uninterested; don't know if it's the heat or what. I miss that fire I had, that excitement. It may have to do with starting my studio class with a new group of students, which generates a nervousness for me.

But I wanted to let you know, that's why I didn't send you my writing this week. Just couldn't get myself to apply any sort of brain power to anything. I'm starting to take ginkgo biloba to see if my memory improves or my energy increases. I'm just a blob, and yesterday I was a slug, in front of the fan. Blob and slug, that's me . . .

FairyCoachMother: Hello blob and slug. Yes, it's the heat. And the fact that your energy is being redirected right now to the start of your class. Be gentle with yourself and give yourself permission NOT to be high on creativity all the time. This is part of the rhythm of everything.

Creativity undulates over all sorts of terrain and sometimes seems to disappear altogether. I believe that people who create consistently are those who relax into the ebb and flow (think of bobbing on the ocean) and allow themselves to rest and rejuvenate after a period of great production. We need to realize that it's normal and BE GENTLE with our creative selves.

ArtForce1: Oh, I'll be alright, but I hate this feeling, and now that I know how good I can feel, it's even less fun than it used to be. Even the *Nevertheless* spell isn't working. I just feel bullied and used up.

FairyCoachMother: Just a thought: you're not pointing your magic wand at your own head, are you? Or zapping that little girl inside? As in, "I'm tired. Nevertheless, I'm going to write," or "I want to sit here and read a book/write my syllabus/watch a schmaltzy Lifetime movie. Nevertheless, I'm going to my studio and paint!"? You don't want writing to feel like a drain, an obligation. You don't even want it to be your "spiritual practice" (maybe one of them) because when you make something into EVERYTHING it turns to dust. It's supposed to. It can't sustain that power.

ArtForce1: Whoops. I was thinking more like, "I'm hot. Nevertheless, I am going to write my prompt for Cheryl . . ."

FairyCoachMother: *Nevertheless* is reserved for nasty things the witch tells you. As in, "You're such a slug! You're just sitting here sweaty and unattractive and you're not even producing anything!" And you say: *Nevertheless*, I'm replenishing myself to do the work. Or, "You're not writing or painting every day! You're not feeling high every day! You should be creating all the time and feeling great! You should be materializing TRANSCENDENT STUFF every day and feeling enlightened!"

And you say: Nevertheless, I'm gentle with my body and my creativity. I honor the times art flows through me, and I honor the times it needs to go underground. I honor my body's need to feel pretty and functional and comfortable, and that it—not you, Witchy Woman!—sometimes needs to be my focus. (I also honor this fan for making me feel cooler.)

A week later I got a note in the mail ...

One of the things my older brother and I used to do (we shared a room until I was eight and he was nine) was one of us lie down on our backs and the other right side up on the edges of our bunk beds, and make faces until we could imagine that the other's chin was their nose, and their tongue and smile were upside down ... we would crack ourselves up for the longest time! Try it!

Hey! It's my upside down smile — it's back!

Editor's note: Portions of the note were obscured by pastry cream and coffee stains, but we believe we've captured the gist.

KEEPING YOUR CREATIVE SPIRIT ALIVE

BY JILL JONES   ART BY MARY HALDEMAN AND SARAH FISHBURN

MARY HALDEMAN

There are seven concepts at the heart of any creative-endeavor successful plan. Internalize these ideas, and your creative spirit will stay lively as you navigate a path to realize your creative dreams.

1. GET INTO THE HABIT

Find "religion" by establishing the habit of working on your creative endeavors regularly. Believe that what you are doing is important. To give creativity the importance it deserves, establish a work schedule and mark appointments in your calendar. Treat the appointment as "sacred time"—an appointment that cannot be broken. Don't do the dishes, fold laundry, write e-mails or watch TV during the scheduled appointment. Just go to your space and create.

2. START THE MORNING RIGHT

Start each day with a creativity connection. This can take many different forms, such as reciting a mantra, lighting incense or candles, organizing supplies at your workspace or taking fifteen minutes to work on something creative. In fifteen minutes you can make a quick collage, write a journal page, take countless photographs or sing four songs in the shower. The particular action we decide to take is not as significant as the meaning we grant to the ritual. Determine what is meaningful to you and practice it each day as a way to stay connected to your creative inner life throughout the day.

Get up early and spend thirty minutes to an hour creating before heading to the office. If you already get up at an ungodly hour to make a long commute, investigate other options to support the creative life. For example,

use mass transit and work on projects during the commute, take supplies to the office to work piecemeal at breaks, or carve out time in the evening to work. Even thirty minutes several times per week starts to add up.

3. TALK BACK TO YOUR SELF-TALK

Negative messages from external sources often outweigh the positive ones, and we perpetuate the abuse through our judgmental self-talk. The exciting news is we can counteract and change our self-talk. Choose to stop believing the bald-faced lies your self-talk uses to trip you up. Start by being skeptical of everything your negative self-talk tells you. Write down answers to counteract the poison and practice them out loud.

4. WORK WITH WHAT YOU HAVE

Everyone has limitations of one type or another—not enough time, not enough money, too many demands from family or work … Writers can work just as well with pencils as they can with platinum-tipped pens, and good art can be made at the kitchen table from recycled materials.

The more important elements needed in the equation are passion, courage, focus, motivation, desire and follow-through. If we think we have to wait until all the stars are aligned and all our ideal conditions are met, we will never move any closer to our goals. Expecting it "all" up front typically leaves us with "nothing."

5. BEGIN AGAIN

Always begin again. If things go poorly on any given day, that doesn't mean all is lost. Go to bed thinking of possibilities for the next day and when you wake up, start again. Learn to work in the middle of things and not wait for inspiration or a magical burst of energy. The muse will visit more often if you are working on a regular basis.

6. DO WHATEVER IT TAKES

Some things in life will understandably stop us in our tracks—serious illness, death of a loved one, natural disasters. Extreme conditions may require a pause, and then we find a way to go on. It is our challenge to find a way to keep working and do whatever it takes to advance our goals as we meet the day-to-day challenges of living. All our ideal conditions won't ever be met at the same time, so we are challenged to work with what we have at the time and keep moving forward.

Be honest and stay open to opportunities to learn about yourself and the world. Be forgiving and understanding while encouraging yourself to dream bigger, work harder and take more creative risks. Love your creative expressions and do whatever it takes to keep at it.

7. ESTABLISH A SUPPORTIVE NETWORK

Surround yourself with creative, positive, supportive influences, and weed out the ones that are negative and toxic. Find other people who enjoy working together and learning. Take classes that support your goals while offering a venue for meeting people who share your interests. For an extra boost consider working with a creativity coach to help focus and advance your creative aspirations.

Street Games of Boys in Brooklyn, N.Y.
By Stewart Culin
American Journal of Folklore 4 – 1891

The games of which I shall give an account are all boys' games or games in which both boys and girls participate, and were all described to me by a lad of ten years, residing in the city of Brooklyn, N. Y., in games in which he himself had taken part. They are all games played in the streets, and some of them may be recognized as having been modified to suit the circumstances of city life, where paved streets and iron lampposts and telegraph poles take the place of the village common, fringed with forest trees, and Nature, trampled on and suppressed, most vividly reasserts herself in the shouts of the children whose games I shall attempt to describe.

SARAH FISHBURN

Embracing the Unknown

by Terry Lee Getz

Who wants any more mystery or chaos in life than one encounters merely by swinging legs out of bed? Not me! There can be joy in not knowing. After all, we live in a chaotic universe that we can barely understand. Aren't human struggles just exercises in the attempt to control outcomes? How's that working for us?

We prefer the static life so that we know what will happen from moment to moment. We can control our environments to a certain extent and, admittedly, a level of static energy is necessary. Without gravity, we'd be flying around the constellations, all willy-nilly. While kissing Orion sounds intriguing, it's equally nice to consider kissing our significant others more than once in a bazillion light years, by passing chance.

I've attempted over the years to control creativity. This can be done and seems necessary if you sell artwork. Having an art show or exhibit in my future switches on my Auto Listmaker. Auto Listmaker's job is to ensure I have X number of widgets to sell or show by a given date. Auto Listmaker's job is to ensure that I realize I must create or die—as in, starvation. No pressure there!

Is it any wonder that I do not skip to my art table? The obligation of preparing art for a show messes me up—big time. When widget making appears in my future, suddenly I'm fired up to begin that long procrastinated project of cataloguing my book collection. Indeed, those tomes have gone ages without order, not to mention a decent dusting. Widgets require a degree of mass production that bores me, so I crave *One Life to Live*. I haven't watched since Asa was a young man, if he ever was. His grandson Kevin has a son whose name escapes me and is easily only two years younger than his father! Who killed Margaret because she was carrying Todd's baby? Todd looks much too young to have a sixteen-year-old daughter. Before I know it, I'm my own grandpa and I don't remember what a widget is. Mission "Distraction" accomplished!

In an attempt to seduce myself, I displayed my best beads on the coffee table where they screamed for my attention. I looked, I fondled and I held them to the light. Ooohhh, shiny! I arranged them in lines, circles, triangles and intricate patterns defying Euclidian geometry. Hemp to knot them? No. Waxed linen for stringing? No. A pin loom woven strand? No. Exasperated, I bought wallet-busting Soft Flex wire that set me back fifteen dollars for ten yards. What is that stuff, spun titanium?

Holding the end of that wire in one hand and a bead in the other, I experienced paralysis like a scarecrow on a pole—only, without the grin. I'm fifty years old. I've worked with beads since I was a three-year-old, stringing clothesline rope through a plastic bead the size of a doughnut. In fact, my first spoken word was "bead." After six (count 'em) weeks of thinking about bead stringing, I could not string a bead on that wire to save my life. My own blood stung my own eyes as it ran from my own forehead. Here's a six-dollar piece of wire, and here's a round object with a hole in it. *Do something!*

Here's what I did: I whisked all the beads, hemp and linen into the ever after, and took a Xanax and an eighteen-hour nap. I awoke fresh to face a new day, until I remembered the art show and the widgets. I had a thought (dear Joseph, call the media!), "Throw out the widget idea! Stop forcing stuff! Forget the shoppers, the money and the starvation! Just make something! Anything! Who cares?"

Seventeen days before the show. No widgets made. While wandering the house in a trance, I spotted some shrine-like boxes that I've had for five years. Why not just go crazy putting paint on those shrines and get inspired? Indeed, why not? It was better than nothing, so I started applying paint. I laid that paint on and I must say, energy did flow. I mixed up some secondary colors and painted the shrines in complementary colors. They were bright. They had a lot of loose painting on them. The shrines I envisioned as "spirit houses" looked instead like "Pee-Wee's Playhouse." Not that there is anything wrong with "Pee-Wee's Playhouse," other than it exists in an alternate universe. Even in their Pee-Wee-ness, the shrines looked too contrived; they were heavy looking. After I patiently dried the five pieces with my heat gun, I knew that these shrines were not what I wanted. Why, oh why, do the happy accidents I hear other artists speak of never happen to me? (How I hate them.) What could be done to breathe some life into these shrines?

I'd spent a good eight hours painting five shrines, then blow-drying them. I decided to wash paint off the shrines. It's a good thing I took time to dry them before I washed them, because that paint came off easily and irregularly. My method of washing the shrines was as follows: I dunked them into a bucket, thoroughly wetting them. I removed some paint with my hands, some with a scrubber. I then took paper towels and dabbed, swiped and absorbed paint, drying the box as much as possible but not taking all the paint off. The stripped shrines finally looked like something that occurred naturally, especially if you enjoy the look of an orangutan having painted them with its lips and toes and backside. Really natural.

I would like to tell you that this story has a happy ending here: the shrines ultimately looked like they had weathered Egyptian desert winds and tropical rain forest damp, enhanced further by the addition of wonderful, rare and precious found objects that perfectly suited them. At the art show, my friends were astounded by my creative abilities and bowed in the "we are not worthy" gesture that naturally emerges when one is in the presence of creative genius. I behave humbly, as do all the great creators of history, raise my fist in a *Rocky*-esque iconic pose and yell, "Widgets Be Damned!" in exultation. I leave the show with ten thousand dollars in my pocket.

That sounded almost believable, didn't it? Jeepers, I'm good! When it comes to spinning fantasy, I am definitely your huckleberry.

Here's the real story, not nearly so dramatic but with the smidge of reality we cling to whenever possible. I did nothing with the shrines at all (yes, they still mock me). Ultimately, I decided to do wax painting/mixed-media work on stretched canvas. Yes, you heard me right! Working with wax was an entirely new experience for me; in fact, I worked directly from Claudine Hellmuth's excellent book, *Collage Discovery Workshop*. For weeks I'd been falling in love with the twelfth-century Sufi poet Rumi—some obsessions do pay off! My idea to work with spiritual quotes, original photos and a hand-painted Sufi dancer finally felt "right." Claudine's instructions for the wax technique are so specific that my first piece was a success and subsequent experiments proved even more satisfying. As a result, I took six original canvases to the show, selling three. While the financial rewards were appreciated, of more importance to me was the feedback I got from shoppers concerning the spiritual aspects of the work. Some shoppers expressed how the artwork moved them and encouraged me to continue exploring spiritual messages in my visual work.

What started out as failed attempts at beadwork and shrines ultimately became satisfying waxed canvases exploring issues of culture, history, universal spirituality and personal symbology, while exploiting my painting, photographic and design skills. The energy finally turned when I gave up what I "knew" or thought I should do. I love beads, but it wasn't the proper time for me to do beadwork—I had nothing new to bring to it. I've enjoyed embellishing and filling shrines in the past, but the idea felt forced for this show. It wasn't until I was willing to risk and express the new by exploring my current fascinations that my unique ideas and talents melded into a successful creative experience. I risked using a new material, a new surface, a new technique and original photos and painting to produce an entirely new body of work. This process was patiently waiting in the wings while I mentally forced what seemed to be safe and acceptable. This new work was so much more "me" than the other work could have been.

The hard-earned lessons I learned during the process of preparing for the art show included allowing, accepting what came up, experimenting, and releasing expectations of preferred or "suitable" outcomes. I persisted through the frustration of failed efforts and this is perhaps the best lesson for me. I'll remember now to trust my true interests and my Self and have the courage to begin at that point in my process. I will risk plumbing unknown depths that release and fulfill my spirit, and I've arrived at a point in my life, creative or otherwise, where the "unknown" is my preferred orientation.

divine spirit

is present

regardless of our

invitation

TOMATOES

These calendar pages weren't marked up much, so I used the space for therapeutic venting of unhappy thoughts and later covered them with clever gardening ideas that are decidedly more optimistic.

RELUCTANT JOURNALING

by Suzanne Simanaitis

I'm in awe of the amazing journal pages I see published in zines and books—so vibrant, so raw, so alive! Every now and then I think, "Well … maybe I should give journaling another try." But I have a million excuses why not, so the fact is: I'm probably just plain afraid of it.

But when I examine this fear and acknowledge that visual journals come in many flavors, I see that it's mostly a matter of finding my own personal way into the process. As I contemplate journaling, here are some of the concerns that surface and some coping strategies I've developed as a result.

Did I say "coping strategies"? Because I meant "sneaky tricks." Just like I trick myself into eating nutritionally sound yet utterly unappealing bran flakes by disguising them under a fluffy blanket of brilliantly palatable Cap'n Crunch, I've developed a variety of schemes for tricking myself into journaling. Whether you're a reluctant journaler like me or a journaling pro, you might find a tidbit here to add some energy or texture to your process.

I don't have anything worth writing about.

I think of things to write about all day, when I'm at work or in the car or the shower and can't stop what I'm doing to jot it down. Yet when I sit with pen poised over paper, my mind goes blanker than the page in front of me.

TRICK 1: I start with somebody else's words. I copy a juicy quote into my book and then respond to it in writing. This usually provides a smooth segue into writing about whatever is on my mind—otherwise, that quote wouldn't have caught my eye at that moment.

TRICK 2: I let myself bitch. If the first few sentences that come out are whiny complaints about my day, I write them anyway—maybe around the edge of a page—and then I cover them with doodles or collage when I've warmed up. Sometimes you've got to get past some garbage to get to the good stuff.

TRICK 3: I ditch language entirely. Sometimes I'm not in the mood for words at all, but an energetic bout of image wrangling is what I crave. In this case I reach for the nearest magazine and a glue stick, and I wallpaper a page with scraps of torn color. If nothing magic happens, at least the next time I approach my journal I'll have a page all ready to write on that's not blank.

I would die if anyone read my journal.

TRICK 4: I make it extra hard for others to read what I write. Although I have decent handwriting, I dreamed up a strategy recently as I was squinting to read a very important phone number I'd stupidly copied into my address book in fluorescent pink: write stuff in colors that blend in with the background. If I really need to read it back someday, I will manage to decipher my writing, but I can't imagine anyone else will be able to do so.

TRICK 5: I write it and then I nuke it. It's oddly satisfying to deface something I've spent hours working on, especially if it turned out "well." I think there's something very positive about the message it sends to the universe, as in, "Yes, I did this interesting work today, but I don't need to cling to it because there will be more interesting work tomorrow."

A big empty page is too daunting.

TRICK 6: I face small pages instead. Plagued by the twin fears of having nothing to say and not being able to stick with the process, I work in small books—board books or those cute little gift books about kittycats, Zen or cocktails that multiply like bunnies in my junk drawer. This strategy fits with my "small dog/shorter walks" hypothesis of living, as there is a reasonable chance I might actually fill a six-page journal. If I chose a journal that's larger, I cut pages into smaller pages or simple shapes like houses or hands. As with any problem, carving it into digestible, doable segments is a good approach.

TRICK 7: The magic word is tape. Double-stick tape lays down backgrounds, clear packing tape seals everything in, duct tape forms durable hinges—and there's no drying time! With a roll of tape and flaps from my bran flakes box, I build flippy-floppy new pages into an empty journal, extra little panels just big enough to record a Web site address or hide a snippet of writing beneath it. A border of colored masking tape around the edge of a page makes any page seem smaller, and I can write something else on the tape itself, if inspiration strikes.

I start dozens of journals but never stick with one for very long.

I've abandoned several journals after a few entries—I missed a day, and a day turned into a month, and that was the end of that. If the book isn't glued by my side, I don't think about working in it, and I already carry quite enough stuff with me everywhere, thank you very much.

TRICK 8: I carry a spiral-bound calendar book in my purse every day. When it's June 5 do I really need to know what was on the agenda for January 18 anymore? And what about this flurry of lint-covered sticky notes that spills out every time I open the calendar? Out comes the glue stick. I paste useful stuff onto the old pages, like those directions I used to have to MapQuest every time I need them, and now I include the ephemera that describes my days as well as pictures torn out of catalogs and magazines (I am the queen of "I can do that!" reverse engineering). The calendar's spiral binding accommodates all the added layers, and by the time I get to the end of the year I've got a pretty neat document of what was important to me—and isn't that what a journal is supposed to be?

SING

This diminutive journal page includes cereal box cardboard flaps and four kinds of tape, and there's secret stuff written on the back of the big orange letters and under the Loteria card, which no one can see, but I know it's there.

MAYBE

Write in one direction, then turn around and go back the other way to make it tricky for the untrained eye to decipher at a glance.

The Gift
BY GAIL RUSSAKOV

Teaching art at a local high school for twenty-five years was a roller-coaster ride every day. I enjoyed seeing my students discover the thrill of creating something they were proud of when they turned it in. Many would spend all their after-school hours making art as they progressed through the higher-level courses. These students were driven and knew in high school that art would be the focus of their future.

Some were not sure what major to choose when they headed off to college. There was always plenty of drama and disagreements with parents about the course their lives would take in the next four years and beyond. Parents asked me, "Will my child be able to find work and support herself if she majors in art?" A big question for the art teacher.

I pondered this question for a long time and realized I couldn't answer it. But I told my students and their parents that they should be glad to have this incredible gift of love for the arts. They would be better parents by sharing their creative gift, by making Halloween costumes, decorating the home and sharing the magic of making all kinds of things together. The gift allows us to enjoy the beauty of little things and the joy of observing the world around us. The gift would take them into a special world of sidewalk art shows, galleries, museums and imagination.

Oh, yes, and the best part of the gift? It allows them total contentment when spending time alone and creating something that pleases them. Sometimes the gift is put on the shelf when life gets busy. But the gift can be opened whenever we want to open it and need some time to rejuvenate our souls.

STARING DOWN THE IMPOSTOR
BY VICKIE ENKOFF

ART BY JILL JONES, JULIANA COLES AND MARY HALDEMAN

"It is better to have enough ideas for some of them to be wrong,
than to be always right by having no ideas at all."
—Edward de Bono

Jill Jones

smells of Rosemary. Sounds of quail —that maybe like coy
te. Or Lakota Nation. Cemetary of cactus standing
like monumental crosses or squat tombstones. A constant
HUM OF BEES. THE AIR SMELLS CLEAN AS IF
BLOWN IN OFF THE OCEAN. MOLD ALL
OF MY MEMORIES INTO ONE. PACK
IT IN A BALL AND THROW IT BACK
OUT. THIS IS IT. THIS WANTS
TO BE MY LIFE.

Juliana Coles

"Impostor syndrome" is a term coined by Dr. Pauline Rose Clance to describe the condition of not feeling qualified or deserving of the work one is doing, or a sense of inadequacy even though the facts indicate that the opposite is true. Suffering from impostor syndrome means chronic self-doubt and feelings that you do not know all you should know. It is a feeling that you will be caught and will lose everything that you have earned. "Impostors" believe that they do not deserve their success and fear being found out, like they are getting away with something.

People with impostor syndrome attribute their success to luck or other external reasons—not to their own abilities. They are the ones who have trouble accepting compliments and may discount the importance of what they have accomplished.

Impostor syndrome can be found among all types of people, and artists are especially susceptible. It is impostor syndrome that leads us to price our artwork too cheaply or even just give it away. No matter how successful we are, we have difficulty shaking this feeling even while confronting it with facts to the contrary.

People with impostor syndrome are often hard workers and people pleasers. They try to form an acceptable identity so people will approve of them. Unfortunately, getting praise and approval only reinforces these behaviors. Criticism is difficult to take and only maginfies feelings of inadequacy.

Is it difficult to call yourself an artist or a writer? Do you feel like you are bluffing your way through your activities? Once you identify impostor syndrome in your life, there are things you can do to alleviate those feelings.

1. CREATE AN ARTIST'S STATEMENT. Develop a one-or-two sentence description that you can tell people quickly and without hesitation when asked what it is that you do.

2. MAKE A COLLAGE ABOUT YOURSELF AS AN ARTIST OR WRITER. Gather words and images that remind you of your creative goals (getting your work published, having a solo show at a local hangout, earning money via your artistic skills, or even just bringing a certain project to successful conclusion). Hang it in your work area where it can't be ignored.

3. FIND OR START A SUPPORT GROUP WITH OTHERS WHO FEEL THE SAME WAY. Naming the feelings and simply acknowledging that they are not accurate are great steps toward resolving these feelings.

You could start an art group in your community and meet at a coffee shop or scrapping store (ask for permission to use the space, of course), or you could establish an online group to discuss these issues via e-mail. Either way, your group could do collaborative projects, such as an altered book round-robin or an artist trading card swap beginning with the theme "My Inner Critic" and evolving from there.

With a group, you can practice asking questions about things you don't understand so that you get used to showing others that you do not know all the answers. You'll begin to feel more comfortable with topics that are difficult for you.

4. IDENTIFY FEELINGS VERSUS FACTS. Work on your automatic thoughts and challenge them as they come up. Keeping a journal is a good way to work through these. Write down your negative thoughts in a journal, and then underneath, rewrite them in a more positive way. For example:

   Negative: I shouldn't even bother making art—there are so many other artists who can do it better.

   Positive: Everyone has to start somewhere and, with practice, I can produce good art too. It doesn't have to be like someone else's art. It can be whatever feels right to me.

   Negative: I can't sell my art because it's not good enough.

   Positive: I can sell my art because I do what I love and my enthusiasm about my work will be contagious.

5. ASK A FEW TRUSTED FRIENDS TO DESCRIBE YOU AS THEY SEE YOU. It doesn't need to be a dissertation, just a list of eight or ten adjectives would do. You will probably find that other people describe you much more positively than you view yourself, and you'll be surprised at what things people like about you that you would not have considered.

6. VISUALIZE SUCCESS. Write out all the steps you need to take to be successful. Take classes. Read books. Gather missing information. Find mentors. The more you know about the task you have to complete, the easier it is to be successful.

7. IT IS ALL RIGHT TO MAKE MISTAKES. Forgive yourself as you would a friend. No one is perfect and you don't have to be perfect either. You don't have to know everything. The key is to be able to research and locate information as you need it. Remind yourself that you may not know everything, but you are surely smart enough to learn.

8. KEEP AN ACCOMPLISHMENT LOG TO REMIND YOU OF ALL YOUR SUCCESSES—it is hard to discount them when they are in writing. Focus on your strengths and your accomplishments, not your weaknesses and all the tasks that stand before you. Compare each success to your previous work, not to someone else's.

9. KEEP A JOURNAL OF HOW YOU RESPOND IN STRESSFUL SITUATIONS, the feelings you have, and the negative voices you hear. Then you can write about how you would prefer to respond, whether it is by voicing your opinion or holding back. You can develop a plan for next time and practice different responses to stressful situations until your preferred response comes naturally.

Mary Haldeman

KEEPING MY ENEMIES CLOSE

by ROBIN OLSEN

I'm amazed at the excuses I can come up with not to make art. This makes *no sense* to me because art making is one of the great joys of my life. I began to imagine my negative thoughts as my art demons and realized that it was time to exorcise them. I knew I would be much better off if they were pinned to the wall instead of haunting my thoughts and actions.

Inspired by Susan Shie's spontaneous, journalistic fabric pieces and Jean-Michel Basquiat's raw explosions in paint, I wanted to capture some of those intense feelings as I gave faces to my demons. After finding several artists' quotes that mirrored my feelings, I began to layer and fuse bits of fabric, often grabbing precut scraps that were within arm's reach. Trying to listen to my instincts rather than preplanning, I loaded my workspace with beads, buttons, embroidery floss and found objects, and let the pieces evolve. After doing a large series of them and hanging some on my walls as visual reminders that these are only silly voices in my head, I found that the demons have now evolved into a joyful character series that celebrates the value of playfulness in art.

LAST DAY by Violette

the last day of the
★ WORLD aS We KNoW it! ★

1. Make amends to everyone I've hurt
2. Call up loved ones
3. turn off coffee maker

Don't forget to put on a clean pair of UNDERWEAR!

4. Tell everyone I love them ♥
5. Spend time meditating in Nature
6. have a very good Bottle of PiNoT gRiS handy → with some yummy olives
7. Put my feet in the OCeaN
8. eat some jamoca almond fudge ice cream

I was making a list of things I should do since it was the end of the WORLD and all and the SouND of my mother's voice broke my CONTEMplation! ★

SO YOU'VE CAUGHT THE ZINE BUG . . .

Hey, you've worked your way through this book—congratulations! You've learned a little, you've laughed in all the right places and you've become enthralled with the concept of art zines. But you've run out of book—what now? The way I see it, you're ready to wade, swim or dive headlong into the zine pool, so don your water wings and let's go!

GET YOUR HANDS ON SOME ACTUAL ZINES.

Why not begin with the art zines listed in the Contributors section of this book (pages 139–141)? Drop them a line, send them some mail art and let them know you enjoyed their work! They will be delighted to hear from you. Order a subscription or some single copies to see if this art-zine scene is your thing.

It's highly unlikely that you'd find any zines at your local corporate bookstore, but there are a few independent bookstores, comic book stores, rubber stamp stores and alternative CD shops that stock a small selection of zines on a wide variety of topics (not just art).

Your best bet is to look online. Just pop the phrase "art zine" in your Internet search engine and start surfing. Include a keyword such as "art" or "creativity" in your search term, because there are a gazillion zines out there but only a very small percentage of them are art-related.

Your search may lead you to zine distros (short for "distributors"). Distros are clearinghouses for zines, most of them operating on the same small-business, do-it-yourself, labor-of-love level as the zines themselves. Visiting a distro

is sort of like going to a really good bakery; you might not think you're hungry, but once you catch a whiff you can't stop at just one cookie. Indulge yourself and sample a few! Maybe there is a magical idea-sparking Evel Knievel zine out there for you, too.

CONTRIBUTE WORK TO A ZINE YOU ENJOY.

When you find a zine that resonates with you, see if they accept artwork or article submissions. Many of them do; in fact, they rely on submissions to fill the pages and make every issue lively.

Locate the submission instructions, which should be available in the printed zine itself or at the zine's Web site. This will explain what formats are accepted and where to send them.

If they accept artwork via snail mail, enclose (or better yet, attach) a note stating the title of the piece as well as your full name and e-mail address so the publisher can contact you with any questions. Some zines will mail your stuff back to you after it's been photographed, if you enclose sufficient money for postage.

If the publisher accepts e-mailed image file formats such as .tif or .jpg, be sure to scan or photograph your artwork at a high enough resolution to look good in print—at least 300 dpi. When you create your image file give it a unique file name like YourName_ArtworkTitle.tif so that there can be no doubt about what it is and who sent it.

Big ("real") magazines often send a free copy of the publication to the artists who contribute to it, but unfortunately zines usually do not have the budget to provide that perk. Read the fine print so there are no surprises. Hey, the cost of the zine is a small price to pay to enjoy your fifteen minutes of fame, right?

START YOUR OWN!

Maybe you've got the bug bad and you want to publish a zine. Before you do, ask yourself whether you envision it as a longterm endeavor or a one-time deal. Plenty of noted zine makers specialize in one-shots, special topic zines that are meant to stand alone rather than as part of a series.

Be honest with yourself about your expectations. If you're looking to make a lot of money and become famous, zines are probably not the way to go. All the zine publishers I know do it because they can't *not* do it. The nebulous buzzing in their colorful flower garden minds must be harvested in some way, and directing it onto the pages of a zine is a blessed relief.

The irony is that if the zine becomes successful and you are expected to meet deadlines and act responsibly with other people's money, you may find yourself ill-equipped

to cope. The creative types who thrive on zine making often don't have the slightest inclination toward bookkeeping, database management or customer service. Keep it simple and organize your mailing list as a spreadsheet, so you can print out mailing labels and add columns where you can keep track of who paid how much and when you mailed each order. Your systems will evolve as your business grows.

Selling subscriptions is a can of worms you might not want to open until you're sure that you're going to be able to sustain your zine-making endeavor and you've got the bookkeeping under control. When you sell a subscription, you're selling a promise that you're still going to be publishing your zine a year from now (and that you're still going to have money in the bank to pay that printing bill!). To simplify your record keeping, you may decide to sell only single copies of your zine. Or you can sell set-based subscriptions so that all subscribers get the same group of issues no matter when they join the party.

DETERMINE CONTENT AND LAYOUT.

All zines are put together a little differently and yours will be, too. Here is a place to start, but where you take it from here is up to you.

Zines have more freedom than books to incorporate individuality and express emotions by how the information is presented, and readers usually respond favorably when you let some personality shine through. Write in the voice that comes comfortably for you and have fun laying out the pages—but remember that the distance from "exuberant" to "messy" is microscopic. You are attempting to communicate ideas, so try to keep it legible, will ya?

What to write about is entirely up to you. Some art zines are how-to oriented while others are more about the artistic output and personal views of the publisher. Try a variety of content types in your first issues, see what feels best and what gets the most feedback from your audience, and tweak the mix accordingly.

Pace yourself. Don't exhaust all of your fabulous ideas in the first issue; choose a few and take time to develop them, then add a few new elements to the mix in Issue 2. If you are hoping to include articles by other writers, put the word out early because contributors need time to prepare their stuff and send it to you.

If you plan to photocopy your handwritten or illustrated zine, create your master copy using a juicy black pen. Remember to leave some blank space around the perimeter of each page, becasue copied material doesn't go all the way to the edges.

If you compose your text on a computer or typewriter (a what?), you could do it in columns and cut those into paragraphs or single lines, and glue them onto your master hardcopy layout pages as you please. Print the columns onto sticker paper to make your life easier. Or design entire

CLOCKWISE FROM LEFT: *Dressmaker* (Sonji Hunt), *Chinese Sketch Book* (Elsie Sampson), *My Friends At Fritch Park* (Mary Zan Sweet), *Broken, Chinese Sweatshop, Shopping Queen's Diary* (Elsie Sampson)

pages as electronic files if you have software such as Publisher, PageMaker or Quark XPress.

Images can be tricky. In a black-and-white, high-contrast images work best, but if they are printed too dark or too light it's hard to see what they are. Run test copies to check print quality.

Most zine makers start out by photocopying their publications on a self-serve machine or having the guy behind the counter do it for you (they have stapling and folding machines back there, too). As the circulation increases, it may become cost effective for you to switch to offset printing on a real printing press. For offset you may have to provide your document as electronic files composed in a software package like Quark XPress or InDesign. It's not a casual thing to make this transition, but if you are printing a couple thousand copies it's worth the investment.

PUT YOUR ZINE OUT THERE.

OK, now you've put together a zine. You've slaved away over a hot copier, and you're ready to send those carefully crafted babies out into the world. So, how do you build awareness, you ask?

A Web site isn't mandatory, but it sure doesn't hurt. Using one of the hosting services that offers site-building tools, it's not hard to register a URL (like *www.yourzinetitlehere.com*) and create a simple Web site that shows the cover of your zine, lists what is inside, and explains how it can be purchased.

Find online groups such as the ones at www.yahoogroups.com and www.livejournal.com where like-minded people are already gathered and communicating. If your zine is about a particular aspect of art making (stamp carving, artist/moms, etc.), there are probably a plethora of Yahoo! Groups that discuss your topic, and those folks are your target audience. Word travels quickly through online groups—good reviews and bad—so if you plan to rely on them for free publicity, do your very best to deliver a good product in a timely fashion.

Poke around to find the zine distro Web sites that seem most likely to reach your audience. They usually ask you to mail some sample zines for their review, and if they think their customers will dig your zine, they'll ask you to send more. Like zines, small distros tend to come and go, so proceed cautiously when agreeing to do business.

There are also festivals where zine makers of all types convene to trade, sell, make and talk about zines. A quick Internet search will turn up the details on festivals in Philadelphia, Austin, Portland and numerous other cities.

REMEMBER THE MOST IMPORTANT THING.

Have a good time making your zine. If it's not fun, it's not worth doing. You'll know it's the right path for you when you finally get one issue safely out the door to your customers and your curious mind immediately begins planning the next one.

CONTRIBUTORS

TRACI BUNKERS
Traci is a fiber artist whose nimble fingers extend into diverse media. She has shared her interests by teaching at gatherings and conferences across the United States for more than ten years. Her publication, *Tub Legs*, is an art zine that covers photography, visual journals, painting and more. E-mail tublegs@bonkersfiber.com to order.

PAM COFFMAN
A native Floridian, Pam spent many happy hours of her childhood making things in her father's workshop. A late bloomer who started college in 1980, she began her art teaching career when she graduated in 1984 at the age of thirty-six. Through her artwork and teaching, she encourages the concept of purposeful play.

JULIANA COLES
Juliana is an award-winning artist and creative expression teacher. She developed Expressive Visual Journaling® as a creative process and teaches it at workshops around the world. Her visual journals are featured in *Making Journals by Hand* by Jason Thompson and she is a regular contributor to *Tub Legs* zine.

LISA W. COOK
A teacher by day and a mixed-media artist by night, Lisa's artwork can be seen at www.picturetrail.com/lisacook and in numerous publications, including *ARTitude Zine* and *Cloth Paper Scissors*.

WENDY COOK
Wendy has been exhibiting her work since 1986. Her disciplines include painting, photography, book arts, assemblage and jewelry. She has been published in the United States, Canada and the United Kingdom. Her work can be spotted at www.polaroid.com and www.golden-paints.com as well as her own site, www.wendycook.com. Look for Wendy in the documentary *The 1000 Journals Project*.

CHRISTINE COX
Christine is a metalsmith and bookbinder who teaches workshops in her studio in Volcano, California. She authors a column, "the metalchick," for *ARTitude Zine*. Find her workshop schedule and many bookbinding materials at www.volcanoart.biz.

ELIZABETH DUNN
Elizabeth has been involved in paper arts and mixed-media assemblage for well over a decade. Several paper arts magazines have published her artwork and articles, and she has been a guest artist on numerous televised craft shows. Elizabeth teaches dimensional and functional mixed-media projects in Los Angeles, California.

VICKIE ENKOFF
Vickie's publications include *The Organized Studio*, *Creative Choices* and her book, *Art Dreams: Careers for Artists*. She is the busy proprietrix of www.vickieenkoff.com, a Web site that helps people locate resources and be more creative. She also runs a small zine distro where she sells her publications as well as art zines written by others.

RANDI FEUERHELM-WATTS
Randi recently left the silenced canyons of Claremont, California, for the bustling metropolis of Ames, Iowa. If you would like to compliment her on her pert figure, learn more about her visual journaling deck (North Light Books, March 2007) or check out her one-shot zines, visit www.randifeuerhelm.com.

MARILEE FOSBRE
Marilee lives and teaches in the beautiful San Juan Islands of Washington State. She'd love it if you'd e-mail a picture of your Reflection Deck cards to her at mfosbre@aol.com.

CLOCKWISE FROM LEFT: *Play* (Teesha Moore), *Tub Legs* (Traci Bunkers), *Nicaragua One-Shot* (Carla Sonheim), *Brain Waves* (Jill Jones), *Invoke* (Kate and Matthew Lyon), *ARTitude* (Suzanne Simanaitis)

TERRY LEE GETZ

Seeing her poems published in the elementary school paper thrilled Terry Lee, a born writer, beyond the high of huffing mimeograph paper. In her forties she discovered zining and loved the idea of co-mingling her writing with her photography. *Pisces Rising Alchemy for Artists* zine was born. Terry Lee intends to publish a *Best of Pisces Rising* in 2006. Goad her on at www.pisces-rising.com.

SONJI HUNT

A painter and fabric artist living in Milwaukee, Wisconsin, Sonji blogs about her creative process (and other things) at http://sonjisays.blogspot.com. Ask about *Dressmaker Zine*, Sonji's limited-edition handmade art zines that are a vibrant expression of her mad desire to collage with words, found objects and all the tiny visual ideas she collects.

JILL JONES

Jill is an artist, writer, instructor and creativity coach assisting individuals to develop their creative potential. Jill's artwork has appeared in galleries as well as magazines, zines and other forums. She is the editor, publisher and coffee pot washer extraordinaire of a creativity zine called *BrainWaves*. You can reach Jill via www.brainwavesart.com and at BrainWaves Art Studios, P.O. Box 2530, Corona, California 92878-2530.

CHARLOTTE KEMSLEY

Charlotte is a mixed-(up?)-media artist who is originally from Denmark but has lived most of her life in the United Kingdom. You can see more of Charlotte's work at www.picturetrail.com/madder_than_a_hatter, and you can read her ramblings at http://aliceoverground.typepad.com. Consider yourself warned!

NICOLE LANDY

Nicole began as a painter, then learned to use pastels, which opened the floodgates to mixing media—incorporating collage, cardboard and more. As flat objects took on dimension, assemblage was born and with it the desire to incorporate handmade elements. So she learned to work with polymer clay and metal, and she is still learning! Nicole can be reached at nicolelandyart@hotmail.com.

SYLVIA LUNA/SILVER MOON

Sylvia has forged a dynamic "grunge" style involving collage, fabric, beads, metal, wood, polymer clay and lots and lots of paint. She is a longtime contributor to *ARTitude Zine* and her work has been showcased in *Cloth Paper Scissors*, *Mary Engelbreit Home Companion* and other publications. Sylvia lives in Gilbert, Arizona. Visit www.silvermoonstudios.com to see more of her artwork. P.S. I love Steve!

KATE LYON

Kate delights in the pure joy of creating. She has been published in *The Studio Zine*, *Belle Armoire* and *The Art Doll Quarterly*, among other publications. She is the owner of www.studiosblackbird.com, a purveyor of distinctive art materials, and co-owner of Invoke Arts, which produces a line of rubber stamps and publishes a zine called *Invoke (The Spirit of Art)*. Her web site is http://katelyon.com.

MATT LYON

Matt is an artist, musician and programmer who enjoys making things and figuring out how to make them better. He is co-owner of Invoke Arts, and his personal web site is www.postsomnia.com. *Invoke Zine* launched in 2003 when Matt wanted a venue for writing and practicing art direction, and Kate wanted to try to get people to look at things differently. Individual issues of *Invoke* are available at www.invokearts.com.

MARNEY K. MAKRIDAKIS

Marney is the founder and editor of Artella, a lively support network for creative spirits. Works published in *Artella Zine* are the result of collaborations exploring "the waltz of words and art." Marney's initial concept has grown into a sprawling web site that includes art for sale, email discussion groups, contests and numerous resources. For creative eBooks by Marney, visit www.artellawordsandart.com.

BRENDA MARKS

Incorporating layers of imagery, color and texture, Brenda's work often combines nature and kitsch and incorporates strong graphic qualities. Her artwork has been published in national magazines, and she is a regular contributor to *ARTitude Zine*. Brenda lives and creates in Silverton, Oregon. More of her work can be seen at www.brendamarks.com.

LOU McCULLOCH

As senior designer for *Altered Arts* magazine, Lou tries to keep up with all the latest art trends. Lou is the author of *Paper Americana: A Collector's Guide*. Her work has been published in *ARTitude Zine, Altered Arts* and *Cloth Paper Scissors*. You can see more of her work at www.alteredlou.blogspot.com.

CLAUDIA MEDARIS

Descended from Basque shepherds and deeply committed to introversion, Claudia managed to graduate with an art degree without speaking to a soul. A member of the Capolan Exchange, Claudia currently funnels her creative energy into submissions for art zines including *The Studio*, *BrainWaves* and *ARTitude Zine*. She can be contacted at medaris@hotmail.com.

PATTI MONROE-MOHRENWEISER

Patti is a full-time mixed-media lettering artist (and calligraphy maverick) living in southeast Michigan. She is also the author of *No Shelves Zine*, a zine "for those who defy definition." For more information, visit www.beyondletters.com.

COREY MOORTGAT

Corey is an artist, wife and mother who lives in the Seattle, Washington area. She works primarily in collage, with her favorite subjects being old photootographs, nudes, vintage papers and, most recently, her new muse, son Riley. See her artwork at www.picturetrail.com/coreymoortgat and you can read her blog at coreymoortgat.blogspot.com.

ROBIN OLSEN

Robin is inspired by the raw energy of primitive art, graffiti and children's artwork. She works playfully and from her intuition, filling her artwork with color, texture, sparkles and treasures. Robin's work can be seen in galleries and juried shows around the Portland, Oregon area and in national magazines.

PILAR ISABEL POLLOCK

Pilar Isabel is a mixed-media artist and writer living in southern California. A frequent contributor to *ARTitude Zine*, she is currently working on several projects including her second book of poetry and prose. Her first book of poetry, *The Medea Letter*, is in its second edition. For more information, contact pilarisa321@cox.net.

CHERYL REED, PHD

As the senior research analyst of Cats for Change, an organization dedicated to helping creative individuals live their deepest instincts, Cheryl is a writer, teacher and creative coach. To learn more visit www.catsforchange.org or email her at drcreed@catsforchange.org.

GAIL RUSSAKOV

Gail has taught high school art for twenty-five years. She also teaches workshops at art retreats such as Art Unraveled (Phoenix, Arizona) and The Creative Palette (St. Mary's, Georgia). Her collage work has been published in national magazines and displayed in both solo and group shows. Gail's artwork and teaching schedule may be viewed at www.gailrussakov.com.

ELSIE SAMPSON

Elsie enjoys creating works on paper, including her limited edition artist zines and books *Chinese Sweatshop* and *Chinese Sketchbook*. She is originally from Hong Kong and her favorite artform is cooking. Contact Elsie at P.O. Box 981, White Plains, NY 10602 or elsie@chinesesweatshop.com. Visit her website for more information at www.chinesesweatshop.com.

SUZ SIMANAITIS

Suz's bio is on the first page of this book, but now she would like to mention her award-winning publication, *ARTitude Zine.* It's a quarterly independent magazine about art, craft and creativity, and readers swear that its friendly approach and clear instructions actually motivate them to stop dreaming about it and go make some art! Artful correspondence gratefully received at P.O. Box 190, Hawthorn, CA 90251. P.S. There's a surprise waiting for you—yes, *you*—at: www.artitudezine.com/special.htm.

CARLA SONHEIM

In another life, Carla was the art director for *Christianity Today* magazine; for the past five years she has spent her days painting and trying to paint. Her "girls" are featured in a dozen galleries nationwide and may be viewed at www.carlasonheim.com.

SUSAN TUTTLE

Susan is a mixed-media artist with particular interests in collage, assemblage and abstract painting. She resides in Maine, and her artwork may be viewed at www.ilkasattic.com.

VIOLETTE

A Canadian artist born in Morocco to Spanish parents, Violette is a compulsive painter who works in a surge of energy, painting whatever falls beneath her gaze. She resides in British Columbia where her art and life have become inseparable, and she tools around in her Glittergirl artvan. See more of her artwork at www.violette.ca.

ARTWORK ONLY

A big thank-you to the following artists who shared additional zine-published artwork with us:

Debra Bianchi
Nikki Blackwood
Cynthia Carr
Sarah Fishburn
Mary Haldeman
Donna Koepp
Melissa McCobb Hubbell
Julie Sadler
Deb Silva
Mary Zan Sweet

And an additional thank-you to **Jill Jones** *who provided painted backgrounds to be used as a design element frequently throughout the book.*

INDEX

INDULGE YOUR CREATIVE SIDE WITH THESE INSPIRING TITLES FROM NORTH LIGHT CRAFT

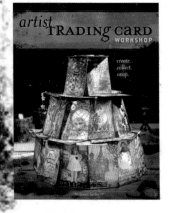

ARTIST TRADING CARD WORKSHOP
Bernie Berlin

Discover the tradition of sharing your work with others as you explore techniques and ideas for using a variety of mediums to make your own artist trading cards. Whatever your creative background, you'll find innovative artistic techniques for making cards, including collage, painting, adding texture, stamping and more. These gorgeous miniature works of art are a great way to introduce yourself to a new medium—and to make friends along the way. The book even offers suggestions for starting your own artistic community to trade techniques and cards.

ISBN-10: 1-58180-848-8
ISBN-13: 978-1-58180-848-3
paperback 128 pages Z0524

COLLAGE UNLEASHED
Traci Bautista

Learn to collage using everything but the kitchen sink with this bright and playful book. Author Traci Bautista shows you there are no mistakes in making art. You can combine anything—from paper, fabric, paint and even paper towels to beads, metal, doodles and stitching to create unique art books, fabric journals and mixed media paintings. The book includes detailed instructions for lots of innovative techniques, such as staining/dying paper towels, freestyle hand lettering, doodling, funky embroidery and crayon transfers. Then you'll learn how to turn your newfound techniques into dazzling projects.

ISBN-10: 1-58180-845-3
ISBN-13: 978-1-58180-845-2
paperback 128 pages Z0024

COLLAGE LOST AND FOUND
Josie Cirincione

Inside *Collage Lost and Found*, you'll learn how to find and use old photographs, memorabilia and ephemera to create collages with a saucy style and a story to tell. Using her own Sicilian background as an example, author Josie Cirincione shows you how to examine your own passions

for inspiration, as well as tips on where to look and what to look for. Then you'll choose from 20 step-by-step projects that use basic collage, jewelry-making and image transfer techniques to make sassy projects to decorate with, wear and give away as gifts.

ISBN-10: 1-58180-787-2
ISBN-13: 978-1-58180-787-5
paperback 128 pages

VISUAL CHRONICLES
Linda Woods & Karen Dinino

Have you always wanted to dive into art journaling, but you're stopped by what to put on the page? Finally, there is a book that comes to your rescue! *Visual Chronicles* is your no-fear guide to expressing your deepest self with words as art, and artful words. You'll learn quick ways to chronicle your thoughts with painting, stamping, collaging and writing. Friendly projects like the Personal Palette and the Mini

Prompt Journal make starting easy. You'll also find inspiration for experimenting with colors, shapes, ephemera, communicating styles, symbols and more!

ISBN-10: 1-58180-770-8
ISBN-13: 978-1-58180-770-7
paperback 128 pages 33442

These books and other fine North Light titles are available at your local craft retailer or bookstore or from online suppliers.